EDWIN MUIR, SELECTED PROSE

EDWIN MUIR
SELECTED PROSE

Chosen, introduced and
with a memoir by

GEORGE MACKAY BROWN

JOHN MURRAY

First published 1987
by John Murray (Publishers) Ltd
50 Albemarle Street
London WIX 4BD

Work of Edwin Muir © Gavin Muir 1924, 1926, 1928, 1935, 1936,
1949, 1954, 1962, 1974
Introduction and Envoi © George Mackay Brown, 1987

The publisher acknowledges subsidy from
the Scottish Arts Council towards the
publication of this volume

Typeset by Rowland Phototypesetting Ltd
Bury St Edmunds, Suffolk
Printed and bound in Great Britain
at the Bath Press, Avon

British Library Cataloguing in Publication Data

Muir, Edwin
Edwin Muir: selected prose.
I. Title   II. Mackay, George Mackay
828'.91208   PR6025.U6

ISBN 0-7195-4394-0

Contents

Acknowledgements

The editor and publishers gratefully acknowledge permission to use Edwin Muir copyright material in this book as follows: Gavin Muir for an extract from 'A Note on the Scottish Ballads' from *Latitudes* and 'Virginia Woolf' from *Transition*; Polygon Books for 'Language' and 'The Place of Poetic Drama' from *Scott and Scotland*; Chatto & Windus · The Hogarth Press for 'The Dramatic Novel' from *The Structure of the Novel*, 'Franz Kafka' and 'Oswald Spengler' from *Essays on Literature and Society*, 'Poetry and the Poet' from *The Estate of Poetry*, extracts from 'Wyre', 'Dresden and Hellerau' and an extract from 'Rome' from *An Autobiography*; and three letters from *Selected Letters of Edwin Muir*; Mainstream Publishing for extracts from 'Glasgow' and 'The Highlands' from *Scottish Journey*.

George Mackay Brown's 'Edwin Muir at Newbattle' is based on an article published in the August 1981 number of *Akros* magazine.

Introduction

When he was a boy at his father's farm at Garth, Orkney, Edwin Muir tells us how he devoured all the reading material he could lay hands on, indiscriminately.

Later, in Glasgow, in the hours he could spare from his clerk's desk, he was intoxicated with ideas: especially those of Nietzsche. The value of other men's ideas, in his case, was that they unblocked his own mind. Swift and turbid the stream came, as can be seen from the essays in his book *Latitudes* (1924). These essays gave him pain when he re-read them much later. One has the impression of a young horse let loose in a spring meadow. Yet, among all the enthusiasms and denunciations of *Latitudes*, one is aware of an eager questing mind. His early essay on the Ballads is a splendid piece: first fruits of an enthusiasm that held him all his life long. At the time of his death, in 1959, he was planning to use his Bollinger award for a full-length study of the Ballads. He held those anonymous poems, along with the work of Henryson, Dunbar, and Burns, to be Scotland's finest achievements in literature.

His next book of critical essays, *Transition* (1926), is interesting if only for the increased lucidity of his prose. His mind was slowly clearing after the ferment of *Latitudes*. Many of his judgements cannot now be faulted, sixty years later: he was appreciative of Joyce; severe on Aldous Huxley; rich in praise of Virginia Woolf's early novels. He could see little of merit in the early Eliot; it was only much later that he arrived at a truer judgement. Even Eliot's criticism seemed to him, though good, flawed in some vital ways.

Did it take courage to write *Scott and Scotland*, a fine-honed ruthless book that held modern writing in Scots to be an aberration: the Reformation and the Bible in English having destroyed the old language and the old unified national culture? For Muir, this book was, as always with him, a quest for the truth; he followed wherever the argument led him. It led, among other things, to a breaking of his friendship with the Scottish poet Hugh MacDiarmid. One might agree with Muir's arguments and conclusions, but feel at the same time that, for reasons of space, he was compelled to leave too much out – for example, he merely nods towards MacDiarmid's own Scots poems, especially the masterpiece 'A Drunk Man Looks at the Thistle'; and these poems to some extent invalidate Muir's conclusions. Only to some extent, for MacDiarmid, in his later long philosophical poems, used English, possibly to reach a wider audience, but also possibly because an impoverished Scots language was too narrow to contain the swoop and scope of his argument.

But in *Scott and Scotland* Muir's prose is much clearer and more incisive than in *Latitudes*. This purity of statement is a process that went on until his last years, arriving at a marvellous lucidity and profundity in his late *Essays on Literature and Society* (1949) and *The Estate of Poetry* (his Harvard lectures).

Scottish Journey (1935) is written in a kind of dream prose. The actuality of Scotland in the political depression of the mid-thirties is palpable; but one has the impression that the man driving the car from Edinburgh – none too well, either; in one way his life was a kind of long skirmishing with the motor-car, as if every car resented the countryman, the lover of horses who was trying to control it – that this traveller through the Borders, Ayrshire, Glasgow, the Highlands, was seeing everything at a remove. There has rarely been such a trenchant exposure of capitalism and industrialism as the chapter on Glasgow in *Scottish Journey*. 'I take my journey back to seek my kindred/ Old founts dried up whose rivers run far on/ Through you and me . . .' At the end of the quest lay Orkney; which, even then, was yielding him the symbols and images of his greatest work, his poetry.

His finest prose work is, I think, *An Autobiography*, the first part of which appeared as *The Story and the Fable* in 1940. (It is a pity, in a way, that he ever relinquished the original title: it is the key to nearly all of his life and work.) There has rarely been a more beautiful evocation of the life of a child. One thinks of parts of *The Prelude*, of

Vaughan and Traherne, *Twenty Years A-Growing* by Maurice O'Sullivan (another island childhood from the Irish Blaskets), 'Fern Hill' and the semi-autobiographical stories of Dylan Thomas. Muir's *Autobiography* has this dream-like quality too, even when the light of common day beats upon it. It is more a series of 'illuminations' than a straightforward life-story. As readers of Muir know well, and are apt to complain over, the dreams sometimes overmaster the writer and his prose, reaching the extraordinary intensity of the series of waking dreams in a London room in the early twenties. It was impossible for him to resist such impulses and images that came to him from the deep sub-conscious treasury of the race. The hard rock of poetry is beginning to show through the shallow soil of 'real life', long before Muir knew that he was, first and foremost, a poet.

When, hesitantly at first, the rhythms of poetry came, in Europe, it was the buried life of his childhood in Orkney that nourished it. One small boy chasing another along an island track, going home from school – all our lives are drifted deep in such idle memories. But little Edwin Muir was the child who ran away in terror. The memory set up resonances, until the great bronze of Homer rang again: Achilles pursued Hector under the walls of Troy.

'In dreams begin responsibilities.' Edwin Muir had many illuminating things to say about our own times. I had thought, until I re-read it recently, that after the first two great movements of *An Autobiography* – Orkney and Glasgow – the book petered out in a series of rather tired chapters; Edwin and Willa's wanderings not at all like the Lawrences' vivid 'hunt of the sun', for example. I was struck, on a recent re-reading, by his insight into the tides and refluxes of European politics before and after the war: the great and the little betrayals, the walls and corridors and baffling dead-ends of the labyrinth.

For Edwin Muir, history seems a kind of deception, and all written historical accounts somehow unsatisfactory, or at best a partial explanation only; the modern times in which he was caught up he sees rather as only one manifestation of the abiding fable; and poetry is the oracular tongue of fable. From those European wanderings come the magnificent late essays, 'The Natural Man and the Political Man', 'The Politics of King Lear', 'Oswald Spengler . . .' There is a poem called 'The Castle' in *The Voyage* collection (1946): the seemingly impregnable castle is betrayed by a 'wizened warder' who opens a little side gate and lets the enemy in. That this image had haunted him for long is evident from the fact that it occurs in his novel, *The Three Brothers*, written much earlier; and that in its turn was based on an actual historical incident, the reduction of St Andrews castle in Scotland, and the murder of Cardinal Beaton, at the time of the Reformation. It may go farther back still, to his childhood on the farm, when 'the great gate' swung open and let in all the evils of time. (That is one interpretation; it is a very mysterious poem.)

Again, a vividly-recorded dream of Muir's tells of the encounter of a splendid heraldic beast and a little soft earth-coloured creature; in the dream the creatures fight over and over again, and the magnificent beast is always victorious – or seems to be – but always the insignificant animal returns, unvanquished, to the fray. It doesn't require much imagination to connect this dream-incident, which later became the poem 'The Combat', with the American onslaughts on Vietnam in the 1970s. Muir's poem was prophetic; it was written some time before the Vietnam war. And yet the poem and the dream probe to the very roots of existence – 'the poor crooked scythe and spade' always outlast 'sceptre and crown'.

The life, the prose, and the poetry are indivisible. It is interesting to note the steps that led to the writing of Muir's greatest poem 'The Transfiguration' (which has been rather coldly treated: T. S. Eliot, for example, omits it from his selection of Muir's verse). In his early teens, Muir was 'converted' in Orkney by a travelling evangelist, caught up with others in a wave of religious fervour. It did not last; yet for a while afterwards the world and its people were invested with a marvellous purity and light . . . It happened again, in Glasgow, years later, when he took part in a May-day Socialist procession. All the people round him, the shabby and the prosperous and the workaday, seemed like transfigured creatures, that age, poverty, and corruption

4

could never touch, essentially. Those moments 'in and out of time' –
recorded in the *Autobiography* – can never be forgotten. Years on, the
magnificent poem 'The Transfiguration' was waiting. In that poem
Muir seems to achieve an ultimate cleansing in his art; the images are
dissolved in light; words and rhythms come close to the perfection of
silence.

There is, alas, no room in a selection like this for specimens of the
Muirs' Kafka translations. They never met each other, but Edwin
out of deep affection and gratitude called him 'dear Franz' in a
sonnet. Minds fructify across generations and oceans, of course,
otherwise literature and art and music would be empty interlude and
ornament. But it is as though Kafka and Muir are brothers in a
deeper sense; Muir worked in that Greenock bone factory, and the
whole episode might have been plotted by Kafka, in rhythm and tone
and image. The essay on Kafka will have to stand for the bond
between them.

Muir wrote excellently on the novel in his early book *The Structure
of the Novel.* There is an especially interesting chapter on the novel of
character – like *Tom Jones* and *Vanity Fair* – which needs space for its
unfolding, and in which time (though always of course present) is of
comparatively small account; and the dramatic novel, like *Wuthering
Heights*, which is narrowly confined to the Yorkshire moors, and in
which time smoulders and breaks out at last into flame, and the
characters 'move in measure, like dancers'.

There is another very different kind of novel, the chronicle, the
greatest being *War and Peace*, which exploits both time and space –
three generations, the huge terrain of Russia – for its unfolding.
While he acknowledges its superiority, as art, to *Pride and Prejudice*,
Wuthering Heights, *Vanity Fair*, one feels that history – great masses of
people, armies on the move, dynasties shaken, cities burning – is (as
they say nowadays) not his scene. The lesser, though still great
novels, are: the lonely figures, or small groups of people interacting,
are closest to 'the fable', and that is where his imagination finds its
chief nourishment.

His own historical novel, *The Three Brothers*, is the least satisfactory

5

of his books. He had free entry into the fable, the mythical past; but he distrusted history itself, and all its cold documentation. 'The historical necessity' so much insisted on by fascism and Marxism seemed to him to be a kind of dark labyrinth in which humanity is becoming increasingly lost.

It has always seemed strange to me, though, that the rich medieval history of Orkney had no appeal for him. It must be that the *Orkneyinga Saga* is too crowded with the ruffians and vaunters he instinctively shrank from. But from Wyre, where he passed his early childhood, he could see Egilsay and the round tower of St Magnus Church – 'it was the most beautiful thing within sight, and it rose every day against the sky until it seemed to become a sign in the fable of our lives . . .' But the life and character of Magnus, the peace-bringer, did not once touch his imagination.

I have chosen a few of his letters, because they show more clearly than the *Autobiography*, or even personal encounters with him, his spontaneous generosity, courtesy, and sweetness of nature. There is one astonishing letter: the nightmare car journey across Czechoslovakia with the mad driver. I include it because it seems to gather into a few vivid words so much of the essence of Muir; the Kafkaesque atmosphere – the farcical Muir-motor car relationship, of which this is another episode – the deep symbolism of the pot of honey – and the wry way in which the episode is related. It happened; it is part of 'the story'; but the fable enters it too, in some mysterious way.

To any reader new to Edwin Muir, it might seem that he dealt only in high seriousness, like Milton and Wordsworth. There are, however, marvellous 'country matters' in the *Autobiography*, chiefly associated with his cousin Sutherland, a kind of island Falstaff, and his aunt Maggie. These, and others, are real Orkney country folk, they can be encountered any day on a road or a seashore; but too, they are a part of the fable, as though they had always been, and always will be.

Is this, or something like this, what Edwin Muir meant when he insisted that he was certain of every man's immortality? Writing about his greatest friend, John Holms, he certainly did not mean a continuance of the personality after death; and Nietzsche's idea of eternal recurrence was at last repellent to him. 'It is your prison that makes you free . . .' Somewhere, in the labyrinth, is a right passage, and the key that opens the last door to the light.

*

I have concluded the book with an essay which gives, perhaps, a glimpse of the Muirs at one of the brief pleasanter stations of their journey through this troubled century.

George Mackay Brown, June 1986

CRITICISM

A Note on the Scottish Ballads

. . . What distinguishes the Scottish peasantry is not only its cradling in the dialect, but a whole view of life, a view of life intensely simple on certain great, human things, but naturalistic, perhaps in a certain sense materialistic. This simple vision of life, of life as a thing of sin and pleasure, passing, but passing with an intense vividness as of a flame, before something eternal, is the greatest thing which Scotland has given to the literature of the world. Everything which obscures the clearness of this vision, making it less simple than itself when it is most simple, is antagonistic to the Scottish genius; and here, and here only, in defence of their naturalism, of this terrific, sad and simple vision of life, the Scots are iconoclasts, and contemptuous of the thing called culture or humanism which in other lands has had such glorious fruits. Knox expressed the national temper when, disdainfully asserting that the image of the Madonna was only 'a bit painted wuid', he threw it into the sea; and Carlyle repeated it on a grand scale in his Dumfriesshire judgements on all the figures which the culture of the West gave into his hands. Carlyle, in genius one of the greatest of all the writers born in Scotland, was in attainment one of the most patchy and immature, simply because he constantly passed judgements on men and cultures foreign to him; judgements which of Scotsmen and Scots culture would have been true, but which of them were valid perhaps only on some intensely human plane, and on every other absurd.

This sense of life and death, of pleasure and sin, of joy and loss, not thrown out lavishly into all the manifestations of life as Shakespeare threw them out, but intensified to one point, to the breaking point where a flame springs forth: that is the sense which has inspired the greatest Scottish poetry: the poetry of Burns, the poetry of the ballads. Burns, it is true, was more nearly than any other

Scottish poet a humanist, and had more than any other a delight in the variety of life; but when he was greatest he came to simplicity, that simplicity of stark, fundamental human things which the ballads more perfectly than any other poetry express. He is not greatest in lines, magical as they are, such as

> Yestreen when to the trembling string
> The dance gaed through the lighted ha',

but in

> And sae I sat, and sae I sang,
> And wistna o' my fate,

or in

> We twa hae paidl'd in the burn
> Frae morning sun to dine,
> But seas between us braid hae roared
> Sin' auld lang syne,

or in

> And I will luve thee still, my dear,
> Though a' the seas gang dry.

The unquenchability of desire, the inexorability of separation, the lapse of time, and all these seen against something eternal and as if, expressed in a few lines, they were what human beings have felt from the beginning of time and must feel until time ends: these things, uttered with entire simplicity, are what at its best Scottish poetry can give us, and it can give them with the intensity and the inevitability of the greatest poetry. The ballads go immediately to that point beyond which it is impossible to go, and touch the very bounds of passion and of life; and they achieve great poetry by an unconditionality which rejects, where other literatures use, the image. In no poetry, probably, in the world is there less imagery than in the ballads. But this, once more, is not the sign of poetic debility, but of a terrific simplicity and intensity, an intensity which never loosens into reflection; and reflection is one of the moods in which images are given to the mind. There is nothing in the ballads but passion, terror, instinct, action: the states in which soul and body alike live most intensely; and this accounts for the impression of full and moving life which, stark and bare as they are, they leave with us. It is this utter absence of reflection which distinguishes them also from the English ballads, not only from those surrounding the name of Robin Hood, which are nothing but simple folk-art, but from really beautiful English ballads such as 'The Unquiet Grave'. There are several Scottish ballads containing, like it, a dialogue between two lovers, the one living and the other dead; but there is none which treats the subject in this way:

> The wind doth blow to-day, my love,
>   And a few small drops of rain;
> I never had but one true love;
>   In cold grave she is lain. . . .
>
> 'Tis down in yonder garden green,
>   Love, where we used to walk,
> The finest flower that ere was seen
>   Is withered to a stalk.
>
> The stalk is withered dry, my love,
>   So will our hearts decay;
> So make yourself content, my love,
>   Till God calls you away.

That is beautiful, and as poetry as perfect in its way as anything in the Scottish ballads; but what a difference there is in spirit and in atmosphere. Here there is retrospection and resignation; but there only the present, the eternal present, and the immediate acceptance of it, exist, and we never escape from the unmixed joy, the absolute pain. There is philosophy in 'The Unquiet Grave', the quality of a great reflective poetry; there is morality in it, the inescapable ethical sense of the English, and that feeling of ultimate surrender which goes always with a genuine morality. But see with what a total lack of moral compensation, or of moral bluntening, or of resignation, or of alleviation – with what a lyrical and unconditional passion the same theme is treated in a great Scottish ballad, in 'Clerk Saunders';

> Is there ony room at your head, Saunders?
>   Is there ony room at your feet?
> Or ony room at your side, Saunders,
>   Where fain, fain wad I sleep?

> There's nae room at my head, Marg'ret,
>   There's nae room at my feet;
> My bed it is fu' lowly now,
>   Amang the hungry worms I sleep.

Or, almost as simple and great:

> O cocks are crowing on merry middle earth,
>   I wot the wild fowls are boding day;
> Give me my faith and troth again,
>   And let me fare me on my way.

> Thy faith and troth thou sallna get,
>   And our true love sall never twin,
> Until ye tell what comes o' women,
>   I wot, who die in strong traivelling?

I do not wish to make any comparison between these two poems, both great in their kind, or to praise one at the expense of the other. I wish merely, what is infinitely more important, to make clear what are the peculiar attributes of the Scottish ballads, and what it is that they have given to the poetry of the world. And it is preeminently this sense of immediate love, terror, drama; this ecstatic living in passion at the moment of its expression and not on reflection, and the experiencing of it therefore purely, as unmixed joy, as complete terror, in a concentration on the apex of the moment, in a shuddering realization of the moment, whatever it may be, whether it is

> I wish that horn were in my kist,
>   Yea, and the knight in my arms neist.

or

> And I am weary o' the skies
>   For my love that died for me.

or

> Yestreen I made my bed fu' braid,
>   The night I'll make it narrow.

or

> This ae nighte, this ae nighte,
>   Everie nighte and alle,
> Fire and sleete and candle lighte,
>   And Christe receive thy saule.

This world in which there is no reflection, no regard for the utility of action, nothing but pure passion seen through pure vision, is, if anything is, the world of art. To raise immediate passion to poetry in this way, without the alleviation of reflection, without the necromancy of memory, requires a vision of unconditional clearness, like that of a child; and it may be said of the Scottish ballad-writers that they attained poetry by pure, unalleviated insight, by unquestioning artistic heroism; and this quality it is that, in the last analysis, makes the very greatest poetry great, that makes 'Lear' great, and 'Antony and Cleopatra'. In Shakespeare and in Dante it is united with other qualities through which its utterance becomes infinitely various and rich; in the greatest of the Scottish ballads there is this quality, and this alone. This, and not the occasional strangeness of their subject matter, is what gives them their magic, a magic of ultimate simplicity, of supernatural simplicity, as in

> O they rade on, and farther on,
>   And they waded rivers abune the knee,
> And they saw neither sun nor moon
>   But they heard the roaring of the sea.

from 'Thomas the Rhymer'. Or, from 'Tam Lin':

> About the dead hour o' the night
> She heard the bridles ring.

There is here nothing but a final clearness of vision which finds of itself, as by some natural, or rather, supernatural, process, an absolute reality of utterance which does not need the image. The thing is given in the ballads and not a simile either illuminating or cloaking it; and this absence of the image has in itself an artistic value, and produces an effect which can not be produced in any other way: it makes the real form and colour of things stand out with a distinctness which is that, not of things seen by daylight, but of those, more absolute, more incapable of being questioned, which we see in dreams. When a colour is set before us in the ballads it has a reality which colour has not in poetry where imagery is used; it has not merely a poetic value, it has the ultimate value of pure colour. This is the reason why the ballad of 'Jamie Douglas' gives us an impression of richness as of some intricate tapestry, though the means are as simple as

> When we cam' in by Glasgow toun
> We were a comely sicht to see;
> My Love was clad in the black velvet,
> And I mysel' in cramasie,

or

> I had lock'd my heart in a case o' gowd
> And pinn'd it wi' a siller pin.

There the qualities of the velvet, the crimson, the gold and silver are seen as they are only seen in childhood, for the first time, and with something solid in the vision of them; something which we have perhaps for ever lost, and which the painters of our day, with their preoccupation with volume, are trying to rediscover; but which was given to the ballad-writers by the sheer unconditionality of their vision, and by that something materialistic in the imagination of the Scots which is one of their greatest qualities.

The art of these ballads may appear to us untutored, rough, falling occasionally into absurdities, and, regarding such things as diction and rhyme, showing a contempt for the perfection towards which all art necessarily strives. But the more we study them the more astonished we must become at their perfection on another side: that completeness of organic form which makes each an economically articulated thing. There is, it is true, a sort of logic of ballad-writing, a technique of repetition, of question and answer, not difficult to handle and handled in some of the ballads far too freely; but in the greatest, in 'Clerk Saunders', 'May Colvin', 'The Lass of Lochroyan', and 'Sir Patrick Spens', the technique is fused in the inevitability of the movement from beginning to end, so that one can see them in one glance as one sees a short lyric. The sensation which these give us is the sensation which can only be given by great conscious art. It is not a matter of the compulsory unity which folk-ballads, sung before a company, must have: for that one need only go to the English ballads about Robin Hood, ballads definitely beneath the level of poetry, which can run on in the style of

> The King cast off his coat then,
> A green garment he did on,
> And every knight had so, i-wis,
> They clothéd them full soon,

for as long as one likes. The difference between that and

> The King sits in Dunfermline toun
> Drinking the blude-red wine

is the difference between a thing seen and shaped by a company of common men in a jovial mood, and a thing seen and shaped by a great spirit, lifted up on the wings of imagination. All these English ballads are timid, ordinary, and have the mediocre happy ending which crowds love. For example, three of Robin Hood's followers, we are told, go down to London, cast themselves on the King's mercy and nevertheless are condemned to death: they are reprieved at the last moment by the Queen. This would not happen in a great Scottish ballad. Johnnie Armstrong, in the ballad of that name, puts himself in the power of the Scots King, and he, too, is condemned to die, but there is no reprieve. The difference in treatment between the two episodes is the difference once more between great poetry, imagined by a heroic and sincere spirit, and second-rate folk-poetry, re-counted by good-natured and insincere men. In the ballads of Robin Hood we are not told, as we are in the Scottish, what must happen, the circumstances being such and such; we are told what the ballad-makers wish to happen. The vulgarity of the happy ending, which has disfigured so much of the greatest English imaginative literature since, making it less great than it should have been, is already full-fledged here. I say vulgarity, for the fault of the happy ending is that it is vulgar; it is a descent from the level of aesthetic vision where tragedy is bearable to that of our ordinary wishes, where it is not; a complete betrayal of truth and beauty at the bidding of an impulse perfectly natural and perfectly common. This surrender negates form by its own spirit, just as the unflinching grasp of aesthetic vision holds and fulfills form. The dependence of style upon this thing is in poetry absolute; and it is by virtue of their spirit, and because they are conceived and executed entirely on the level of aesthetic vision, that the Scottish ballads are opulent in examples of great form and great style, as, to quote an example of both:

> Why does your brand sae drop wi' blude,
>   Edward, Edward?
> Why does your brand sae drop wi' blude,
>   And why sae sad gang ye, O?
>
> O I hae kill'd my hawk sae gude,
>   Mither, mither;
> O I hae kill'd my hawk sae gude,
>   And I hae nae mair but he, O.

To write poetry such as that, not only an exquisite sense of form was needed, but a great and sincere spirit, an elevated and intrepid mind.

Looking back on that tremendous world mirrored in the Scottish ballads, one is tempted to exclaim, What a culture there must have been once in that narrow tract of land between Edinburgh and the Border, and what a tragedy it was that its grand conception of life as a thing of sin and enjoyment, of life and death, of time and eternity, realized in pure imagination, was turned by Knox and the Reformation into a theology and a set of intellectual principles! But Knox's work has been done; it has not been undone; and time alone will show whether it ever will be. Certainly only a people who saw life so intensely as a matter of sin and pleasure, of sin in pleasure and pleasure in sin, could have accepted with such passion a theology which saw life as a thing of transgression and damnation. There is something unswerving and, however we may dislike and deplore it, heroic, in the theology as well as the poetry of Scotland. A burning contemplation of things which take men beyond time made her equally the destined victim of Calvinism and the chosen land of the ballads. But of that national tragedy it is idle now to speak. To those, however, who deny that a poetry so immediate as that of Scotland, so entirely without reflection, can be great human poetry and of value in a world in which so much of the dignity of the life of men is involved in the fact that they are capable of reflection, one can only say that a mighty reflection, or rather something more than a reflection, is implied in the very spirit of the ballads, a reflection on supreme issues which is unerring and absolute and has come to an end; a reflection not tentative, not concerned with this or that episode in a poem, with this or that quality, moral or immoral, or with the practicality or impracticality of life but of life itself, finally and greatly; a reflection which is a living vision of life seen against eternity: the final reflection beyond which it is impossible for the human spirit to go. In the Scottish ballads life is not seen, as it is seen so often in English imaginative literature, as good and bad, moral or immoral, but on a greater and more intense level, as a vision of sin, tremendous, fleeting, always the same and always to be the same, set against some unchangeable thing. In this world, so clear is the full vision that pity is not a moral quality, but simply pity; passion not egoistic, but simply passion; and life and death have the greatness and simplicity of things comprehended in a tremendously spacious horizon. It is idle to attribute this simplicity, which is a capacity for seeing things as they are eternally, to the primitiveness of the existence which the ballads mirror. Life was at that time, as it has been always, complex, a mystery not easily to be pierced. If one wishes to see what mere simplicity without an over-powering vision of life seen *sub specie aeternitatis* can do, one can go in any case to the folk-ballads surrounding Robin Hood. But the Scottish ballads have something which ordinary folk-poetry has not, that great quality, that magnanimity about life, inadequately called philosophic, which Arnold found in Homer.

Whether the Scottish genius will ever return to some modified form of the ballad as its preordained medium it is useless to consider to-day. Probably Scottish writers are fated herafter to use English, and to use it, taking all things into account, not with supreme excellence. But it is difficult to avoid two conclusions: that the ballads enshrine the very essence of the Scottish spirit, and that they could have been written only in the Scottish tongue.

Scottish Literature

Scottish literature, considered linguistically, may be divided into Early Scots, Middle Scots, and Anything At All. The first two periods exhibit a certain homogeneity of language and as a result of that a definite style; the third, which began tentatively with Knox (the first Scotsman to write good English prose), and definitely with the acceptance of the English translation of the Bible, signalizes a disintegration of the language of Scottish literature and the disappearance of a distinctive Scottish style. Scotland continued to produce writers, but they wrote in a confusion of tongues ranging from orthodox English to the dialects of the various Scottish districts. The only speech which they did not continue to use was Scots, for that had disappeared. Consequently, since some time in the sixteenth century Scottish literature has been a literature without a language. Middle Scots survived Sir David Lyndsay for a while in the lyrics of Alexander Scott and Montgomery. But a little later Drummond of Hawthornden was already writing in pure English, and since then Scottish poetry has been written either in English, or in some local dialect, or in some form of synthetic Scots, such as Burns's, or Scott's, or Hugh MacDiarmid's. Scottish prose disappeared altogether, swept away by Knox's brilliant *History of the Reformation* and the Authorized Version of the Bible.

The reasons for this disintegration of the language of Scottish literature are controversial, and I have no space to enter into them here. But it is clear that the Reformation, the Union of the Crowns, and the Union of the Kingdoms had all a great deal to do with it. I must confine myself, however, to certain of its consequences. The prerequisite of an autonomous literature is a homogeneous language. If Shakespeare had written in the dialect of Warwickshire,

Spenser in Cockney, Ralegh in the broad Western English speech which he used, the future of English literature must have been very different, for it would have lacked a common language where all the thoughts and feelings of the English people could come together, add lustre to one another, and serve as a standard for one another. A common language of this kind can only be conceived, it seems to me, as an achievement continuously created and preserved by the highest spiritual energy of a people: the nursing ground and guarantee of all that is best in its thought and imagination: and without it no people can have any standard of literature. For this homogeneous language is the only means yet discovered for expressing the response of a whole people, emotional and intellectual, to a specific body of experience peculiar to it alone, on all the levels of thought from discursive reason to poetry. And since some time in the sixteenth century Scotland has lacked such a language.

Every genuine literature, in other words, requires as its condition a means of expression capable of dealing with everything the mind can think or the imagination conceive. It must be a language for criticism as well as poetry, for abstract speculation as well as fact, and since we live in a scientific age, it must be a language for science as well. A language which can serve for one or two of those purposes but not for the others is, considered as a vehicle for literature, merely an anachronism. Scots has survived to our time as a language for simple poetry and the simpler kind of short story, such as 'Thrawn Janet'; all its other uses have lapsed, and it expresses therefore only a fragment of the Scottish mind. One can go further than this, however, and assert that its very use is a proof that the Scottish consciousness is divided. For, reduced to its simplest terms, this linguistic division means that Scotsmen feel in one language and think in another; that their emotions turn to the Scottish tongue, with all its associations of local sentiment, and their minds to a standard English which for them is almost bare of associations other than those of the classroom. If Henryson and Dunbar had written prose they would have written in the same language as they used for poetry, for their minds were still whole; but Burns never thought of doing so, nor did Scott, nor did Stevenson, nor has any Scottish writer since. In an organic literature poetry is always influencing prose, and prose poetry; and their interaction energizes them both. Scottish poetry exists in a vacuum; it neither acts on the rest of literature nor reacts to it; and consequently it has shrunk to the level of anonymous folk-song. Hugh MacDiarmid has recently tried to revive it by impregnating it with all the contemporary influences of Europe one after another, and thus galvanize it into life by a series of violent shocks. In carrying out this experiment he has written some remarkable poetry; but he has left Scottish verse very much where it was before. For the major forms of poetry rise from a collision between emotion and intellect on a plane where both meet on equal terms; and it can never come into existence where the poet feels in one language and thinks in another, even though he should subsequently translate his thoughts into the language of his feelings. Scots poetry can only be revived, that is to say, when Scotsmen begin to think *naturally* in Scots. The curse of Scottish literature is the lack of a whole language, which finally means the lack of a whole mind.

This division in the Scottish consciousness is so far-reaching that if I were to enumerate all its consequences this chapter would go on to the end of the book. So I shall confine myself to some of its effects on poetry. I have often wondered why the Scots, who have shown themselves in the past to be a theological and speculative race, should have produced scarcely a single verse of good religious or meta-physical poetry. In the seventeenth century Scotland was steeped in theology far more thoroughly than England. Yet England produced the religious and metaphysical poetry of that time, and against Donne, Marvell, Traherne, Vaughan, Herbert and Crashaw, all that Scotland could show was a metrical version of the Psalms which is a curiosity.

Now it is clear that there are other reasons for this poverty of Scots poetry in the seventeenth century and since than the fact that Scotsmen already felt in one language and thought in another, and that there was no effective collaboration between their sensibility and their intellect. It will be best, therefore, to consider some of these reasons first. One of them was without doubt the strict Calvinism of the Scots, which was adverse both to the production of poetry, and to poetry itself. Another was the complete prohibition put upon poetic drama by the Reformers just when it seemed on the point of developing; a prohibition which killed not only the drama itself, but also a great number of other forms of poetry which normally flow from it. This matter of dramatic poetry, indeed, or rather the lack of it, was probably crucial for Scottish literature; and if that is so, then the Reformation truly signalized the beginning of Scotland's decline as a civilized nation. For poetic drama occupies a central and decisive position in the development of the three literatures which I mentioned at the beginning of this essay. In all three, English, French and German, poetry and literature in general came to self-consciousness in a great burst of poetic drama, and this achievement of self-consciousness influenced all the poetry that followed, whether lyrical or dramatic: poetry was thenceforth more aware of itself and more capable of essaying the non-dramatic major forms. If one compares the lyrical poetry of England before Shakespeare, of France before Racine, and of Germany before Goethe, with the lyrical poetry after them, one can see quite clearly this difference in self-consciousness. Before the change one finds the simple lyric with all its natural thoughtless grace; after it one finds a body of poetry lyrical in form, but expressing all the richness and complexity of experience as it is known to the self-perusing mind. To take a simple instance, the English metaphysical poetry of the sixteenth century with its 'dialogue of one' would be inconceivable without the rich dramatic 'dialogue of many' which preceded it or was contemporaneous with it.

The strict surveillance of Calvinism, then, and the consequent failure of Scotland to achieve poetic drama, may partly account for the fact that in her poetry since the sixteenth century she has failed to rise above the level of the simple lyric; why she has no Donne, no Baudelaire, no Hölderlin; why she has no romantic poet even of the rank of Beddoes; and why the only poetry with which hers can be compared is early medieval poetry such as that of Walter von der

Vogelweide, and the folk-song which belongs indiscriminately to all peoples.

Yet allowing for Calvinism and the failure to achieve poetic drama, we do not completely account for the poverty and simplicity of Scottish poetry since the sixteenth century, for at the time when Scotland had a homogeneous literary language – when thought and feeling, in other words, could come to equal collision in the poet's mind – she did produce one major poem, Henryson's 'Testament of Cresseid', and a number of poems by such writers as Scott and Montgomery and the anonymous authors of the lyrics in the Bannatyne and Maitland collections, which in their intricacy of movement and fusion of feeling and thought foreshadowed the English metaphysicals. Take this verse from one of Alexander Scott's lyrics:

> Luve is ane fervent fire,
> Kendillit without desire:
>> Short plesour, lang displesour,
> Repentance is the hire;
>> Ane puir tressour without mesour:
> Luve is ane fervent fire.

Then take this from one of Burns's songs:

> But a' the pleasures e'er I saw,
>> Tho' three times doubl'd fairly,
> That happy night was worth them a',
>> Amang the rigs o' barley.

The first of these verses is written by a man who thinks and feels with equal intensity, on the same plane and in the same language, so that the thought heightens the feeling and the feeling the thought; while the second is a mere effusion of thoughtless emotion, with a commonplace judgement tagged on to it exalting feeling at the expense of everything else. If Burns had wished to express his real judgement on that night among the rigs of barley he would have turned to English, as he did in 'Tam o' Shanter' in the one passage where he makes a serious reflection on life. Everybody knows it:

But pleasures are like poppies spread,
You seize the flow'r, its bloom is shed;
Or like the snow falls in the river,
A moment white – then melts for ever;
Or like the Borealis race,
That flit ere you can point their place;
Or like the rainbow's lovely form
Evanishing amid the storm.

I had often wondered why Burns suddenly dropped into English at this point, and for a long time I put down the whole passage as an unaccountable blemish, until I saw that it was the touch that made the poem perfect, the one serious reference that gave all the rest proportion. The point to be noticed, however, is that when Burns applied thought to his theme he turned to English. The reflection in this passage is neither deep nor original, but in the context it is quite adequate. And it is clear that Burns felt he could not express it in Scots, which was to him a language for sentiment but not for thought. He had no language which could serve him equally for both.

When emotion and thought are separated, emotion becomes irresponsible and thought arid. When they are separated so radically that they require two separate languages to express them, the first takes on very much the aspect of an indulgence and the second of disapproval. Scottish poetry is therefore largely emotion, and Scottish criticism has been until quite recent and degenerate times largely condemnation. They are alike in this, that they are equally without standards; for where poetry is written in a variety of dialects with no central language as a point of reference, it is impossible to evolve a criterion of style (there is no standard of Scots poetic style); and where criticism is divorced from sensibility, and consists in the mere elaboration or application of theories, it would in any case fail to judge poetry on genuine literary principles, even if such a criterion existed. Criticism, like poetry, requires a union of emotion and intellect, and where that union is broken criticism comes off as badly as poetry itself. So that in both provinces the division in the Scots mind and the Scots language has had disastrous effects. The worst thing that can be said about Scottish poetry and Scottish criticism is that they never come together, either in general or in the mind of the writer. And until Scotland has a common language for its prose and poetry, its thought and feeling, this evil must continue.

THE PLACE OF POETIC DRAMA

At an earlier stage in this essay I advanced the theory that poetic tragedy represents a crucial stage in the literature of a people, and that by means of it poetry becomes self-conscious, which is another way of saying that it becomes mature. I pointed to the literatures of England, France and Germany in justification of this generalization. It will be generally agreed that the greatest age in all three literatures was an age of poetic tragedy. Goethe held that poetic tragedy was the greatest of all literary forms, and considered the writing of it the highest activity of which any man was capable. I am not concerned with such speculations, however, but rather with the fact that poetic tragedy produces a change in any literature into which it enters, and that literature becomes a different thing after it from what it was before it.

Most of the poetry which precedes poetic drama is of three kinds, lyrical, didactic, and narrative. The first generally expresses a single emotion with the associations appropriate to it; the second is made up of moral reflections touched with feeling and sometimes interspersed with allegory; the third is frequently semi-dramatic, like Chaucer's *Troilus and Criseyde* and Henryson's *Testament of Cresseid*, but the narrator is always present as a directing agent, and the dramatic characters do not have complete independence in the working out of the action. Narrative poetry comprises some of the greatest that has ever been written, including that of Homer, Dante, Chaucer, Spenser, Milton and Wordsworth; and it would be idle to speculate whether it is or is not as great a form as poetic tragedy. Its scope is more extensive than poetic tragedy; like that it generally contains both dramatic and lyrical elements; but it may contain many others as well; it may be purely interesting or purely descriptive, point a moral, invent fanciful episodes of no dramatic relevance, and use any device in general which comes under the category of story-telling. The historical importance of poetic tragedy is that it can do none of these things; that it confronts the poet immediately with a typical human situation, and compels him to work it out to an end. That situation is, by the very terms of poetic tragedy, a conflict, either a simple conflict between two definite opposing powers, or a complex one into which several powers enter; and the poet has to take every side in turn and state each with the utmost force and objectivity. This is never a cold and judicial act; it is much more like 'a sustained passion of self-obliteration, though identification with the creatures of the imagination,' to quote from Mr Middleton Murry's book on Shakespeare. That is to define the dramatic process too violently, however; but it is at least a process in which both the mind and the imagination are put to their utmost stretch in an objectivization of all the conflicting powers of the poet, not in peace or suspension, but in intense action. The result is a unique act of self-consciousness, perhaps the most comprehensive act of self-consciousness possible to the human mind outside of mystical contemplation. An act such as this changes the point of gravity of poetry; that is no longer the simple lyrical point, but rather a point determined by a balance between several contending orbits, each of which may be regarded as lyrical, each as a partial expression of the imagination, but given its place and its value in an action working towards an end. This act is, then, compared with simple lyrical utterance, an assertion of self-consciousness: it may even be, as Mr Middleton Murry says, a 'spontaneous utterance of the undivided being.' But that is not a question into which I can enter here, for this is not an inquiry into the nature of tragedy, but into the problem of Scottish literature; and all that I wish to bring out is that poetic tragedy marks a great increase of self-consciousness in any literature in which it appears, and that a literature which lacks it probably lacks something which is necessary for the supreme kinds of poetry.

As for what a literature loses by missing the phase of poetic tragedy, that is impossible to compute, and must depend largely on supposition. It is likely to lack metaphysical poetry, the 'dialogue of one', and all the forms of poetry in which feeling is set against feeling and the intellect enters as a comparative or critical factor. It is also likely to lack a varied and comprehensive language. 'We are to recollect,' says Coleridge, 'that the dramatist represents his characters in every situation of life and in every state of mind, and there is no form of language which may not be introduced by a great and judicious poet, and yet be most strictly according to nature.' Coleridge pointed this out to refute 'a general and mistaken notion that because some forms of writing and some combinations of thought are not usual, they are not natural'; but it has also another bearing, that is, on the vocabulary of poetry. Coleridge says that 'there is no form of language which may not be introduced' by the dramatic poet; and it seems to me that this cannot be postulated of any other kind of poet, lyrical, didactic, or narrative. In the Elizabethan and Jacobean age the English language was employed for poetry with a flexiblity and lavishness which it never achieved again, and which it cannot achieve in any age which lacks dramatic utterance. Yet the dramatic use of poetry by the Elizabethans also enriched the general vocabulary of English poetry, and made it an instrument for kinds of poetry which it could not have produced otherwise. This is a truism, but it is necessary to insist upon it in any consideration of Scottish poetry, which never knew this change at all. What we see in Scottish poetry after the sixteenth century is accordingly a gradual impoverishment of the vocabulary of poetry, an impoverishment which may be judged most clearly by comparing the language of Dunbar with that of Burns. The Scots speech not only became localized; it thinned to a trickle.

We cannot say now whether Scotland would have had a dramatic literature had the Reformation never taken place, or had it taken a different form. The only considerable example of dramatic art that has come down to us from the sixteenth century is Lyndsay's *Ane pleasant Satyre of the Three Estaitis*, which was first produced in Cupar either in 1535 or 1540, and was afterwards presented in Linlithgow and Edinburgh. It is a morality play, containing such characters as King Humanity, Wantounness, Placebo, Sandie Solace, Flattrie, Chastitie, Divyne Correctioun, and so on; but the characters are drawn with great lifelikeness and spirit, and the dramatic skill of the whole is remarkable; for Lyndsay, though a mediocre poet, seems to have been an excellent playwright. J. H. Millar, in his neglected *Literary History of Scotland* says, referring to this play: 'In literature, as in politics, it may be that the "might-have-beens" are illegitimate, as they are futile. But to wonder how the course of Scottish drama might have run if the external conditions had been analogous to those that prevailed in England is certainly a tempting, and perhaps after all an innocent, speculation. That these conditions were, unhappily, very different in the two countries is well known. The Reformation in England helped to pave the way for the Elizabethan drama. In Scotland it was hostile to almost every form of art, and fatal to that which finds its home on the stage. The old sports and pastimes of the people were suppressed with a heavy hand. "Robert Hude", Lyttil Johne, the Abbot of Unreason, and the Quene of the May, were ostracized both in burgh and to landwart. For well-nigh a hundred and fifty years the desolating influence of a gloomy and intolerant fanaticism brooded over the country; and, while it permanently deprived the people of forms of amusement which might have developed into something really worth developing, it did little to abate the national appetite for drink and fornication. If we may judge by Lyndsay's *Satyre*, no nation could have shown a fairer promise of playing a worthy part in the dramatic revival which is the glory of English literature at the end of the sixteenth and the beginning of the seventeenth century.' He praises Lyndsay for the dramatic propriety of the action in this play, and the vividness with which the characters are represented. This praise is reasonable, as well as the contention that miracle and morality plays must have been common in Scotland, though Lyndsay's *Satyre* is the only example that has survived, except for a brilliant fragment by Dunbar or some unknown hand. One can say, from the evidence of the *Satyre* and the correlative evidence, that the germ from which a drama might have sprung existed in Scotland. After the change represented by the Reformation that drama could not develop; if the Reformation had never happened it might have developed, or it might not: that is all that we can say about it. But in support of the first supposition can be advanced the strong gift for dramatic statement which is shown in another large sphere of Scottish literature: that is the Ballads. The best of the Scottish Ballads are more dramatic than the English, a fact which can probably be explained by the fact that the English dramatic sense found an outlet in a different and much more comprehensive form, and that the Scottish dramatic sense did not. The whole grammar of the greatest Scottish Ballads is dramatic, a sort of simplified question and answer. We come across it again and again. In *Clerk Saunders:*

> 'Is there ony room at your head, Saunders?
>   Is there ony room at your feet?
> Or ony room at your side, Saunders,
>   Where fain, fain, I wad sleep?'

> 'There's nae room at my head, Margret,
>   There's nae room at my feet;
> My bed it is fu' lowly now,
>   Amang the hungry worms I sleep.'

In *The Daemon Lover:*

> 'What hills are yon, yon pleasant hills,
>   The sun shines sweetly on?' –
> 'O yon are the hills o' Heaven,' he said,
>   'Where you will never won.' –

> 'O whaten-a mountain is yon,' she said,
>   'Sae dreary wi' frost and snae?' –
> 'O yon is the mountain o' Hell,' he said,
>   'Where you and I will gae.

> 'But haud your tongue, my dearest dear,
>   Let a' your follies a-bee,
> I'll show you where the white lilies grow,
>   In the bottom o' the sea.'

In *The Lass of Lochroyan:*

> 'O wha will shoe my bonny foot?
>   And wha will glove my hand?
> And wha will bind my middle jimp
>   W' a lang, lang linen band?

'O wha will kame my yellow hair,
    With a haw bayberry kame?
And wha will be my babe's father
    Till Gregory come hame?' –

'Thy father, he will shoe thy foot,
    Thy brother will glove thy hand,
Thy mither will bind thy middle jimp
    Wi' a lang, lang linen band.

'Thy sister will kame thy yellow hair,
    Wi' a haw bayberry kame;
The Almighty will be thy babe's father
    Till Gregory come hame.'

If I were to go on quoting, I should never stop. It is true, of course, that this method of question and answer is as much narrative as dramatic: in the last resort a means of telling a story. But though this is so, it has at its best a genuine dramatic power quite apart from its narrative intention, as in

I'll show you where the white lilies grow
    In the bottom o' the sea,

and in

The Almighty will be thy babe's father
    Till Gregory come hame.

I have said that there can be no dramatic poetry except in a language in which the poet can both think and feel, and the Ballads bear out this contention; for they are almost the only Scottish dialect poetry extant in which the poet both thinks and feels in the dialect he uses. Scottish folk-song is pure feeling; but the Ballads express a view of life which is essentially philosophic, though completely devoid of reflection. The dramatic apparatus in them is extremely simple and rudimentary, it is true, and capable of presenting only the most direct contrasts; but for its purpose it is perfectly effective. All that I wish to show, however, is that the disposition to dramatic presentation existed in Scotland on a general scale, and that it might plausibly have found utterance in poetic tragedy if the Reformers had not radically discouraged it. Scotland's dramatic power seems to have gone, in the seventeenth century, into controversy of the dullest but most violent kind, producing such monstrosities as *The Causes of the Lord's Wrath against Scotland, The Poor Man's Cup of Cold Water,* and *Eleven Points to bind up a Believer's Breeches.* In such conflicts there is no catharsis, and no making towards a unity: there is mere division, and nothing but division.

Virginia Woolf

The historian writing fifty years hence of the literature of to-day will find in it a certain note of inhumanity. He will speak of our hostility to mankind, and he will remark how different Mr James Joyce's attitude to his characters is from that of Scott, for example, or Jane Austen. A thorough dislike of their creations characterizes, indeed, the majority of modern novelists. Mr Joyce hates and scorns his characters; Mr Huxley's inspire him with disgust or with ill-natured laughter; Mr Lawrence hews his down right and left in the name of his 'dark god'; Mr Stephen Hudson submits his, most severe test of all, to a scrupulous intellectual scrutiny. These writers do not accept the character as an end in himself; he is always a means to them; he is always on a different plane from the mind which evoked him. The contemporary novelist does not walk through his crowds, on easy terms with them, good and bad, as Fielding and Thackeray walked through theirs. He is not among the works of his hands, but detached from them; he watches their movements as a scientist might watch the progress of an experiment. Jane Austen, we feel, is always at the excursions and tea parties she describes; she is one of the characters, the least observed and most observant of all. But this can scarcely be said of Mr Joyce, or Mr Huxley, or Mr Hudson, even when they are portraying figures clearly autobiographical. There is always detachment in their spirit, a certain hostile watchfulness, a barrier of conscious or unconscious irony. They do not meet their characters on the same level as we should, if we were given the chance.

It may be said of Mrs Woolf that she does meet her characters on this level. She accepts them as ends; she accepts them, that is to say, as people of the same status and existing in the same dimension as herself. She might walk into her novels and be at home in them. She stands in the same relation to her characters as almost all the chief

English novelists have stood to theirs. Her attitude, like theirs, is eminently practical, tolerant, appreciative, intelligent; it has the good sense and sagacity of the English prose tradition.

The point is important, for an easy coming and going between the mind of the novelist and the world he creates has characterized the bulk of great fiction. It characterizes all the Russian fiction we know; it characterizes French fiction to the time of Flaubert; it has characterized English fiction up to Mr Joyce and Mr Lawrence. The advantage it gives to the novelist is clear. It endows his imaginary world with an everyday actuality, a toughness which will stand wear and tear. It insensibly inclines us to the useful illusion that all we are reading about is actual; and when we once believe that, the background of the world will fill in readily behind it, as it fills in behind the happenings we hear of in actual life. But for the artist himself the pragmatic attitude has deeper virtues. If it does not make his imagination more profound, it makes it, at any rate, more dependable, sets it working more thoroughly. His relation to his characters being horizontal, being, that is to say, on the same plane if in one important respect not the same, as the relations of the characters among themselves, he will understand their reactions to each other more naturally and feel them more concretely than he could if he were surveying them from a height, if he were sinking his mind into them instead of sharing it with them. For this practical, everyday, distinctively prose way of approaching the theme perhaps the best term is intelligence. It is not a purely intellectual quality; it consists rather in the use of the intellect and the imagination in a comprehensive but commonsense way, as if, exercised on imaginary situations, they were being exercised on the actual problems of life.

The quality of intelligence Mrs Woolf has in a high degree. It is to be seen equally and is of the same quality in her novels and in her volume of essays, *The Common Reader*; for intelligence works by the same means, whatever theme may confront it. All the notable English novelists of the past have possessed it; the only contemporary novelist, besides Mrs Woolf, who has it in a striking degree is Mr E. M. Forster. Mr Joyce lacks it completely. He has a powerful, erratic intellect, but it is the differentiated intellect of the artist; it is hardly concerned at all with what is normal, expedient, practicable, but simply with what is, whether it should be humanly possible or impossible. Mr Joyce has objectified magnificently his personal world, but it is not a world in which we could live, and to him that is, indeed, a matter of no concern. Yet it is a matter of the first importance in the actual world, and an imaginative work which ignores it ignores something essential; that work may have truth, but it will not be an approximate image of the truth. Mrs Woolf's novels are an approximate image of the truth. The world she shows us is not of such vast dimensions as Mr Joyce's, but it is on a perfect scale: there are all the elements in it that there are in any of the worlds we actually live in, and there is, moreover, a perpetual reference to the world itself, the modern world which looms behind and makes possible our smaller, personal worlds.

Width and justice of comprehension are chiefly necessary in the writer who tries to grasp all these implications and strives to make the picture complete. They were shown in Mrs Woolf's first novel, *The Voyage Out*; they were shown still more remarkably in *Night and Day*. Nothing was more striking in these first two books than the undeviating sobriety of treatment, the absence of facility, the resolve to take all the factors into account and to be just to them all. The convention of the novel is accepted. The author, we feel, has resolved to take the novel as it is, and to make it do all that up to now it has done. In *The Voyage Out* she uses among other methods that of Chekhov. That book is still a little tentative, but *Night and Day*, which followed it, remains in some ways the finest of Mrs Woolf's novels. In depth, in meaning behind meaning, some of the scenes in it are superior to anything else written in our time. The meeting between Denham and Rodney on the Embankment, the description of Katherine's aimless wanderings through London on the evening that she broke her appointment with Denham, the Hilbery household, the delightful but pathetic irrelevancies of Mrs Hilbery: these, brought intimately together in the book as they would be in life, give us the sense of the rich variety of existence which only Mrs Woolf's predecessors in the English novel can give. Certain complex effects which were once characteristic of the English novel, effects in which comedy and tragedy jostle, have been almost entirely lost in our time. Sterne was perhaps the first great prose master of them; Scott is full of them; by Dickens they are exploited freely but crudely. The conversation between Bartoline Saddletree and Davie Deans about the trial of Effie is a perfect example of this style; but we find it again and again in Scott; it is an element in almost all his great scenes. Nothing perhaps can give us a stronger sense of the reality of the situation we are reading about than this juxtaposition of the comic and the tragic. We feel that the writer has seen all its aspects, even the most unexpected, that his imagination has not been canalized by the theme, but is free and can move as it wills. Intelligence once more, the taking of all the factors into account, produces these imaginative juxtapositions; and in *Night and Day* it is Mrs Woolf's intelligence that recreates them. There are dull passages in the book; the various threads of the story are not gathered up, do not become dramatic, until we are a quarter of the way through, but once gathered up, they are never released until the end; the growth and development of the complex of situations is steady. One character after another is caught into the action; and it leaves none of them what they were before. The easy course, the short cut, is never taken; everything is worked out anew. For comprehensiveness of understanding the author has never surpassed *Night and Day*. Yet we feel, regarding Mrs Woolf's later works, that there is something lacking in it: the satisfaction of the artist working within conditions shaped for herself. The given conditions, it is true, are scrupulously observed; but we feel them as a compulsion on the writer; they are too impersonal; they have not been resolved into a completely individual means of expression. *Night and Day* is a book which a writer might execute, submitting to the form rather than finding complete expression through it.

In the small volume of short stories, *Monday or Tuesday*, the experimentation with form began which later gave us *Jacob's Room* and *Mrs. Dalloway*. It is tentative, but lighter, more buoyant, than anything Mrs Woolf had written before. *Jacob's Room* was a great advance; its plan was admirable; the recreation of a figure through memories and associations was a suggestive and perfectly valid device. The book contains several beautiful scenes, but it is not sure, like Mrs Woolf's earlier and like her later work; it has a good deal of the sentimentality which so often comes out of the mind along with a first attempt to express something in it which has not been expressed before. When the artist tries to liberate his essential emotion towards experience, at first he is likely to liberate a great deal more along with it, until in this new kind of expression he learns to distinguish what is essential from what appears so. *Jacob's Room* has a more living quality than Mrs Woolf's earlier work, but it is less critical. *Mrs. Dalloway* is the most characteristic work Mrs Woolf has written. It is so unlike *Night and Day* that they can hardly be compared. It has not the earlier book's finely dramatic development or its intensity; but it is more organic and in a more living sense, it is infinitely more subtle in its means, and it has on all its pages, as *Night and Day* had not, the glow of an indisputable artistic triumph. As a piece of expressive writing there is nothing in contemporary English fiction to rival it. Shades of an evanescence which one might have thought uncapturable, visual effects so fine that the eye does not take them in, that only in the memory are guessed at from the vibration they leave in passing, exquisitely graded qualities of sound, of emotion, of reverie, are in Mrs Woolf's prose not merely dissected, but imaginatively recon-structed. All that in the earlier novels was analyzed is resolved in *Mrs. Dalloway* into evocative images. There is nothing left of the stubborn explanatory machinery of the analytical novel. The material upon which the author works is the same as before, but it has all been sublimated, and, although the psychology is subtle and exact, no trace remains of the psychologist.

And Clarissa had leant forward, taken his hand, drawn him to her, kissed him, – actually had felt his face on hers before she could down the brandishing of silver-flashing plumes like pampas grass in a tropic gale in her breast, which, subsiding, left her holding his hand, patting his knee, and feeling as she sat back extraordinarily at ease with him and light-hearted –

all in a clap it came over her, If I had married him, this gaiety would have been mine all day!

How much more exact that is than analysis could be! It is more exact, for the ebb and flow of the imagery, the rhythm of the sentence, follow the course of the emotion. First we have Clarissa's effusion of uncontrolled, blind emotion evoking the image, 'the brandishing of silver-flashing plumes'; then the emergence from it to a recognition of diurnal reality, reported rather than described, 'leaving her holding his hand, patting his knee'; and finally in the accelerating pace with which the sentence ends, the sudden thought that if she had married him! It is exquisitely done.

Then there is the passage, too long to quote, in which the sound of the bells of St Margaret's, which 'glides into the recesses of the heart, buries itself in ring after ring of sound, like something alive which wants to confide itself, to disperse itself, to be, with a tremor of delight, at rest,' is wedded in Peter Walsh's mind with the image of Clarissa in her house, so that when 'the sudden loudness of the final stroke' comes, it seems to be tolling 'for death that surprised in the midst of life, Clarissa falling where she stood in her drawing room. No! No! he cried. She is not dead!' The mood that Mrs Woolf catches here is quite beyond the reach of the psychological, analytical method; yet how perfectly it is conveyed. But more striking perhaps than either of these is the description of Clarissa sewing her green dress:

Quiet descended upon her, calm, content, as her needle, drawing the silk smoothly to its gentle pause, collected the green folds together and attached them, very lightly, to the belt. So on a summer's day waves collect, overbalance, and fall; collect and fall; and the whole world seems to be saying 'that is all' more and more ponderously, until even the heart in the body which lies in the sun on the beach says too, That is all. Fear no more, says the heart. Fear no more, says the heart, committing its burden to some sea, which sighs collectively for all sorrows, and renews, begins, collects, lets fall. And the body alone listens to the passing bee; the wave breaking; the dog barking, far away barking and barking.

The transition here is daring, but wonderfully successful. While Mrs Woolf is describing the falling of the waves, we never forget Clarissa sewing. The greater rhythm as it were accompanies the less, and it brings into the room where Clarissa is sitting its serenity and spaciousness. There is something in the ritual of sewing, a memory of another rhythm buried deep within it, which an image such as this, so unexpected, so remote, reveals to us. The rhythm of the prose is exquisitely graded; it has profited, one feels, as prose may, whether poetry may or not, by the experiments which have been made in vers libre: in the daring and fullness of the metaphors it has a remote indebtedness to Homer. There is no English prose at present, except Mr Joyce's, which in subtlety and resource can be compared with it.

In a novel like *Mrs. Dalloway*, where the sensory impressions are so concretely evoked and are so much more immediate than they were before, a sort of rearrangement of the elements of experience insensibly takes place. In the traditional novel we have on the one hand the characters and on the other the background, each existing in a separate dimension, and the one generally more solid than the other. Sometimes the environment reacts strikingly on the characters, as for instance in *Wuthering Heights* and in Mr Hardy's Wessex novels, but the reaction is not complex and continuous. It is indicated rather than treated, and the character and the background retain their peculiar values. But in *Mrs. Dalloway* they are more intimately connected; the one merges into the other; the character is suffused by the emanations of the things he sees, hears, feels; and almost inevitably what is presented is a complex of life, of which character and background are elements, both animate, rather than the living character stalking among inanimate things. The characters in *Mrs. Dalloway* are real; they have their drama; but the day and the properties of the day move with them, have their drama too; and we do not know which is the more real where all is real – whether the characters are bathed in the emanations of the day, or the day coloured by the minds of the characters. The result is less akin to anything else attempted in the novel than to certain kinds of poetry, to poetry such as Wordsworth's which records not so much a general judgement on life as a moment of serene illumination, a state of soul. What nature is in *The Prelude* London is in *Mrs. Dalloway*, a living presence, a source of deep pleasure. The mood in which this presence is felt is perhaps the farthest removed from the dramatic, realistic mood. In *Night and Day* the chief thing is the action of the characters upon one another; in *Mrs. Dalloway* it is their intimate daily life with all the things which make it up and have reference only to themselves, but which are nevertheless more certainly their being than their actions are. Mrs Woolf is not concerned in *Mrs. Dalloway* with the character, which is shown in action, in crises (and novels are consequently full of crises), but with the state of being. To give it its value she catches it at a particularly fortunate moment, at a moment of realization; but the means are justified and are, indeed, the normal means of art. To reveal character the novelist concentrates on crises, comic or tragic, leaving untouched the vast, inert mass of experience: in concentrating on the daily existence when it is most significant Mrs Woolf is in a different way obeying the same principle, the principle, indeed, of all imaginative art.

The Common Reader, in which Mrs Woolf's mind deals with figures familiar to us all, shows it perhaps at its best. Her themes range from Chaucer to Conrad, from George Eliot to the Duchess of Newcastle, and in them all she shows the intelligence and practicality of temper of the critic. She has the informed enthusiasm which criticism should never lack but which is tending to disappear from it; her judgements have admirable breadth. The one important quality of the critic which she lacks is the power of wide and illuminating generalization. She holds the scales even, as she does between her characters in *Night and Day*; she uses her sensibility as she uses it in *Jacob's Room* and *Mrs. Dalloway*. It is the same mind, and we never doubt its competence to deal with anything which it fixes upon.

The Dramatic Novel

Next we must consider another form of the novel which, like the novel of action, demands a strictly developed plot.

This is the dramatic novel. In this division the hiatus between the characters and the plot disappears. The characters are not part of the machinery of the plot; nor is the plot merely a rough framework round the characters. On the contrary, both are inseparably knit together. The given qualities of the characters determine the action, and the action in turn progressively changes the characters, and thus everything is borne forward to an end. At its greatest the affinity of the dramatic novel is with poetic tragedy, just as that of the novel of character is with comedy. The dialogue in the most intense scenes in *Wuthering Heights* and *Moby Dick* is hardly distinguishable from poetic utterance; the most memorable figures in *Vanity Fair* and *Tom Jones* are always on the verge of becoming purely comic figures like Falstaff or Sir Toby.

But in all its forms the dramatic novel need not be tragic, and the first novelist who practised it with consummate success in England – Jane Austen – consistently avoided and probably was quite incapable of sounding the tragic note. The instance may seem strange, but it is only so in appearance. The art of Jane Austen has a more essential resemblance to that of Hardy than to Fielding's or Thackeray's. There is in her novels, in the first place, a confinement to one circle, one complex of life, producing naturally an intensification of action; and this intensification is one of the essential attributes of the dramatic novel. In the second place, character is to her no longer a thing merely to delight in, as it was to Fielding, Smollett and Scott, and as it remained later to Dickens and Thackeray. It has consequences. It influences events; it creates difficulties and later, in different circumstances, dissolves them. When Elizabeth Bennett and Darcy meet first, the complexion of their next encounter is immediately determined. The action is set going by the changing tension between them and by a few acts of intervention on the part of the other figures; and the balance of all the forces within the novel creates and moulds the plot. There is no external framework, no merely mechanical plot; all is character, and all is at the same time action. One figure in the pure comedic sense there is in the book, Mr Collins. Mr Collins has no great effect on the action; he is an end, not a means and an end at the same time; he remains unchanged throughout the story. There are other pure comedic elements; for example, the permanent domestic tension between Mr and Mrs Bennett. But in most dramatic novels such figures and combinations are to be found. Hardy has his peasants to give relief and an additional emphasis of proportion to the action; they serve somewhat the same purpose as a sub-plot without being one. The real power of the Wessex Novels lies of course elsewhere, in the development of a changing tension making towards an end. If the chief power of *Pride and Prejudice* does not reside in that, at least half its power does.

The plot of *Pride and Prejudice* is very simple. 'Why, my dear,' says Mrs Bennett in the first chapter, 'Mrs Long says that Netherfield is taken by a young man of large fortune from the north of England.' The mood of expectation is aroused; the young man arrives, and from that moment everything begins to move forward. Bingley is accompanied by his friend Darcy. There are visits and parties. Bingley – easy, good-natured, and impulsive – falls in love with Jane Bennett, and is ready to commit himself at once in spite of his distaste for her family; but his friend advises him against it and persuades him to leave the neighbourhood. Meanwhile Darcy discovers that he has fallen in love, against his judgement, with Jane's sister, Elizabeth; and after struggling against his inclination for a while, proposes in terms which she feels compelled to reject with some indignation. Certain things have happened meanwhile to create an aversion in her mind against Darcy. She has been repelled by his pride; she suspects that he has tried to alienate Bingley from her sister; and she has believed damaging stories about him. After the rejected proposal she receives a letter from Darcy which convinces her that she has been unjust. This is the crisis of the action, the Aristotelian middle of the plot. Everything thus far has moved towards it, but now everything moves towards a different end, determined by it. Darcy is seen to be the reverse of what Elizabeth had thought him; and the punctiliousness which before had made him appear absurd and disagreeable, now, in better circumstances, makes him pleasing. By his agency Bingley is restored to Jane, and Elizabeth, her feelings towards him describing the full circle, becomes his wife.

Where this plot differs from the plot of a novel of action is in its strict interior causation. The first aversion of Elizabeth for Darcy was inevitable because of the circumstances in which they met, because Darcy was proud of his social position and Elizabeth encumbered by her unpresentable family, and because they were people of such decided character that they were certain to dislike each other at the beginning. Elizabeth is true to the candour of her mind in believing Darcy to be cold, haughty and vindictive; she is equally true to it later in acknowledging that she is mistaken, and in changing her opinion. The action is created here by those characters who remain true to themselves; it is their constancy which, like a law of necessity, sets the events moving; and through these they gradually manifest themselves.

The correspondence in a novel of this kind between the action and the characters is so essential that one can hardly find terms to describe it without appearing to exaggerate; one might say that a change in the situation always involves a change in the characters, while every change, dramatic or psychological, external or internal, is either caused or given its form by something in both. In this respect the dramatic novel stands apart both from the novel of action and that of character. There is a hiatus between the plot and the characters in both; there should be none in the dramatic novel. Its plot is part of its significance.

But if in *Pride and Prejudice* a change in the situation involves a change in the characters, the propriety and truth of the progression, in other words of the plot, is of the first importance. That progression will be inevitable on two planes. It will have an inner truth in so far as it traces the unfolding of character, and an external truth inasmuch as it is a just development of the action. Or rather, the identity of these two aspects of truth will here be complete, as it is in no other kind of novel. The novel of character, as I shall try to show later on, is concerned immediately only with the outside show of reality, and it implies beneath, not something corresponding to that, but something relatively incongruous with it. The novel of character brings out the contrast between appearance and reality, between people as they present themselves to society and as they are. The dramatic novel shows that both appearance and reality are the same, and that character is action, and action character.

Both these divisions of the novel may have equal aesthetic truth, then, but it is the identity with itself of the dramatic conception that gives its plot such organic and overpowering significance. Nothing in that plot is left out, or assumed. It may contain antithesis, but no mere contradictions. It will be logical in so far as the characters have something unchangeable in them which determines their responses to one another and to the situation. It will have a progression which is at once spontaneous and logical inasmuch as the characters will change, and the change will create new possibilities. This spontaneous and progressive logic is the real distinguishing feature of the plot of the dramatic novel. Everything does derive from factors stated and unalterable in the beginning; but at the same time the terms of the problem will alter, bringing about unforeseen results.

Both these elements, the logical and the spontaneous, necessity and freedom, are of equal importance in the dramatic plot. The lines of action must be laid down, but life must perpetually flood them, bend them, and produce the 'erosions of contour' which Nietzsche praised. If the situation is worked out logically without any allowance for the free invention of life, the result will be mechanical, even if the characters are true. It is this logic without invention that makes Merimée's tales so curiously lifeless and negative in spite of their fine characterization. His figures exist only in relation to the situation;

they are equal to its requirements; they have no life beyond it. The immediate circumstance depresses a lever, and the action of the figures is prompt and absolutely complete. But these figures have no freedom to choose, to reflect, or even to postpone. Their will does not oppose, or even consider the action they are about to do; they are totally within it, like unreflecting animals. There is no dramatic tension in *Colomba* or *Carmen*; there is only action. The progression is logical, but it is not free; it has not the movement of life.

Some of Hardy's novels have the same fault in a much lesser degree. 'The characters', Mr Forster remarks, 'have to suspend their natures at every turn, or else are so swept away by the course of Fate that our sense of reality is weakened . . . Hardy arranges events with emphasis on causality, the ground plan is a plot, and the characters are ordered to acquiesce in its requirements. His characters are involved in various snares, they are finally bound hand and foot, there is a ceaseless emphasis on fate, and yet, for all the sacrifices made to it, we never see the action as a living thing as we see it in *Antigone*, or *Berenice*, or *The Cherry Orchard*. The fate above us, not the fate working through us – that is what is eminent and memorable in the Wessex novels.' 'There is some vital problem', he says again, 'that has not been answered, or even posed, in the misfortunes of *Jude the Obscure*. In other words, the characters have been required to contribute too much to the plot; except in their rustic humours, their vitality has been impoverished, they have gone dry and thin.' No doubt necessity is too obviously stressed in the Wessex novels, and Hardy's reply to all questions is premature and far too sweeping. Certain vital problems are never posed; yet Mr Forster overstates Hardy's defects. He overlooks the immense power of invention which gives the Wessex novels a living movement in spite of the encroachments of the plot.

When freedom is overstressed the effect is equally false. There is a notorious instance of this in *Jane Eyre*, a novel which just misses being truly dramatic. Jane loves Rochester, but she will not live with him while his wife is alive; this is the real dramatic problem. All Jane's character, all that should of necessity decide the direction of

45

the action, is summed up in her refusal to go against her conscience. The story should have been worked out to the end on this assumption. Instead, Charlotte Brontë has the insane Mrs Rochester conveniently burned to death; she defeats fate, she defeats Jane, making her qualities irrelevant and meaningless, by introducing an accident containing a very curious mixture of amiability, cruelty, and nonsense. Up to this point the story has been worked out dramatically; afterwards it is arranged by the author. In the plot of a dramatic novel a falsehood like this is a fundamental one, affecting the whole – action, characters, everything. In *The Newcomes* Thackeray, 'by a most monstrous blunder . . . killed Lady Farintosh's mother at one page and brought her to life at another.' We hardly notice it; we do not care much what becomes of the plot. But Charlotte Brontë could not make a single false move in the plot of *Jane Eyre* without giving a wrong direction to the whole book. She made a resounding one, and the result is calamitous.

Wuthering Heights is more totally impressive than either *Jane Eyre* or *The Return of the Native*, because the balance between necessity and freedom is held more tautly, and therefore more evenly, and proportion is won through the very intensity of the strain which these two forces impose on each other. How strictly the plot was worked out the reader may learn from a valuable little essay by an anonymous writer, published by the Hogarth Press.* Here it is shown that the framework of necessity, legal and temporal, within which the action was to take place, was carefully worked out by the author. To see after this how spontaneous, how free from disfigurement by the plot, the action is, he has only to turn to the book itself. All on the one side seems to be freedom, all on the other is necessity. Catherine and Heathcliff act of their own will, and their action is perfect freedom; yet at the same time they are figures in a tragedy whose terms and end are ordained from the beginning. The progression in both dimensions is unerring, and it is one progression.

To return to *Pride and Prejudice*, the foreknowledge of this progression can be very powerfully felt in the account of Elizabeth's

* *The Structure of Wuthering Heights*, by C. P. S. (The Hogarth Essays).

first meeting with Darcy. This is how Jane Austen describes it:

Elizabeth Bennett had been obliged, by the scarcity of gentlemen to sit down for two dances; and during part of that time, Mr Darcy had been standing near enough for her to overhear a conversation between him and Mr Bingley, who came from the dance for a few minutes to press his friend to join it.

'Come, Darcy,' said he, 'I must have you dance. I hate to see you standing about by yourself in this stupid manner. You had much better dance.' . . .

'You are dancing with the only handsome girl in the room,' said Mr Darcy, looking at the eldest Miss Bennett.

'Oh! she is the most beautiful creature I ever beheld! But there is one of her sisters sitting down just behind you, who is very pretty, and I dare say very agreeable. Do let me ask my partner to introduce you.'

'Which do you mean?' and turning round, he looked for a moment at Elizabeth, till catching her eye, he withdrew his own and coldly said, 'She is tolerable, but not handsome enough to tempt me; and I am in no humour at present to give consequence to young ladies who are slighted by other men. You had better return to your partner and enjoy her smiles, for you are wasting your time with me.'

Mr Bingley followed his advice. Mr Darcy walked off; and Elizabeth remained with no very cordial feelings towards him. She told the story, however, with great spirit among her friends; for she had a lively, playful disposition, which delighted in anything ridiculous.

This chance encounter starts the train of incidents which lead to Elizabeth's marriage to Darcy, and as it is narrated we are made to feel a premonition of something like this. In its tentativeness, it informs us that it is a step merely, implying not merely a succession of scenes, but a development. If we compare it with a typical incident in *Vanity Fair*, we shall see the difference. The passage describes Becky Sharp's first meeting with Sir Pitt Crawley.

The shutters of the first-floor windows of Sir Pitt's mansion were closed – those of the dining-room were partially open, and the blinds neatly covered up in old newspaper.

John, the groom, who had driven the coach alone, did not care to descend to ring the bell; and so prayed a passing milk-boy to perform that office for him. When the bell was rung, a head appeared between the interstices of the dining-room shutters, and the door was opened by a man in drab breeches and gaiters, with a dirty old coat, a foul old neckcloth lashed round his bristly neck, a shining bald head, a leering red face, a pair of twinkling grey eyes, and a mouth perpetually on the grin.

'This Sir Pitt Crawley's?' says John, from the box.

'Ees,' says the man at the door, with a nod.

'Hand down these 'ere trunks, then,' said John.

'Hand'n down yourself,' said the porter.

'Don't you see I can't leave my hosses? Come, bear a hand, my fine feller, and Miss will give you some beer,' said John, with a horse-laugh, for he was no longer respectful to Miss Sharp, as her connection with the family was broken off, and she had given nothing to the servants on coming away.

The bald-headed man, taking his hands out of his breeches pockets, advanced on this summons, and throwing Miss Sharp's trunk over his shoulder, carried it into the house.

'Take this basket and shawl, if you please, and open the door,' said Miss Sharp, and descended from the carriage in much indignation. 'I shall write to Mr Sedley and inform him of your conduct,' said she to the groom.

She was shown into the dining-room by the porter.

Two kitchen chairs, and a round table, and an attenuated old poker and tongs were gathered round the fireplace, as was a saucepan over a feeble sputtering fire. There was a bit of cheese and bread, and a tin candle-stick on the table, and a little black porter in a pint-pot.

'Had your dinner, I suppose? It is not too warm for you? Like a drop of beer?'

'Where is Sir Pitt Crawley?' said Miss Sharp majestically.

'He, he! *I'm* Sir Pitt Crawley. Reklect you owe me a pint for bringing down your luggage. He, he! Ask Tinker if I aynt. Mrs Tinker, Miss Sharp: Miss Governess, Mrs Charwoman. Ho, ho!'

These two passages are fairly typical of Jane Austen and Thackeray, and the difference between them is salient. It is that Jane Austen's scene can only be completed by other scenes to which it is leading up; while Thackeray's is in a sense complete in itself. We know the characters in it immediately and altogether, because at the start they behave typically, as their generalized selves, and there is nothing for them but to keep on doing so. We will not know Elizabeth and Darcy, however, until the action has revealed them to us. The scene from *Pride and Prejudice* is not merely one which may, but one which must be followed by others. These, moreover, must be unlike it, rather than of the same quality: a differentiation of the particular, not a repetition of the typical, as the scenes in the novel of character are.

This being so, however, those scenes postulate an end. The reader is gradually led to a consciousness of this end; but to the writer it is known from the beginning, and it is a vague apprehension of this, perhaps, not consciously recognized by us, that gives to the action of a story like *Wuthering Heights* that enigmatic significance which we can never analyze. When Emily Brontë is describing an intermediate scene, the whole compass of her characters' lives, all that they have been, all that the future has in store for them, is involuntarily implied in it. Her plot must have been in her mind as a complete pattern from the beginning, and the characters must have existed there, not in their diurnal, invariable form, but in movement, in their entire changing transit through time. Thackeray's characters, on the other hand, being perpetually complete and perpetually the same, might well have been herded loosely in his mind; there is no tension within them or in the action into which he puts them. There is this tension in dramatic characters; the tension between their completeness seen as fate, and their progression seen as development. In the very conception of them there is the problem of time. Time surrounds Becky Sharp, it is true; but it reveals Catherine Earnshaw. It is the element in which she unfolds and in which finally her fate is consummated. The end in the dramatic novel is therefore of extraordinary significance; not merely a rounding off of the story as in *Vanity Fair*, but the final illumination. It is the end not only of the action, but of the characterization; the last touch which gives finality and completeness to the revelation of the figures. The people of the character novelist, as they live in a state of perpetual completeness, are not in need of this final touch. His plot need not be complete from the beginning, simply because his characters are complete at the beginning.

The end of any dramatic novel will be a solution of the problem which sets the events moving; the particular action will have completed itself, bringing about an equilibrium, or issuing in some catastrophe which cannot be pursued farther. Equilibrium or death, these are the two ends towards which the dramatic novel moves. The first, for various reasons, generally takes the form of a suitable marriage.

So much at present for the temporal progression and the end of the dramatic novel. Coming back to *Pride and Prejudice* we may take up now the other respect in which it diverges from the character novel; its confinement to a narrow scene, and to one complex of life. We shall find this concentration of the area of action in almost all dramatic novels. We find it in Hardy, in Emily Brontë, in *The House with the Green Shutters*, even in *Moby Dick*, where though the stage is vast, it is in a sense unchanged: there is no escape from it. The reason for the isolation of the scene in the dramatic novel is obvious enough. Only in a completely shut-in arena can the conflicts which it portrays arise, develop, and end inevitably. All the exits are closed, and as we watch the action we know this. There is no escape into other scenes, or if there is we know that they are false exits bringing the protagonist back to the main stage again, where he must await his destiny. The scene here is the framework within which the logic of the action can develop unimpeded, and shut off from the arbitrary interference of the external world. It gives necessity to that logic by defining the limits within which it may work.

Our conclusions may now be summed up generally before we proceed to amplify them. The plot of the character novel is expansive, the plot of the dramatic novel intensive. The action of the first begins with a single figure, as in *Roderick Random*, or with a nucleus, as in *Vanity Fair*, and expands towards an ideal circumference, which is an image of society. The action of the second, on the contrary, begins never with a single figure, but with two or more; it starts from several points on its circumference, which is a complex, not a nucleus, of personal relationships, and works towards the centre, towards one action in which all the subsidiary actions are gathered up and resolved. The novel of character takes its figures, which never change very much, through changing scenes, through the various modes of existence in society. The dramatic novel, while not altering its setting, shows us the complete human range of experience in the actors themselves. There the characters are changeless, and the scene changing. Here the scene is changeless, and the characters change by their interaction on one another. The dramatic novel is an image of modes of experience, the character novel a picture of modes of existence.

Starting from those general conclusions, we may now tentatively approach another. Keeping our eyes on those two divisions of the novel as they are, we must needs believe that neither could give us its characteristic sense of human variety if it did not observe its limitations. Without its shut-in arena the one could not evoke such a range and absoluteness of experience in its figures. Without the unchangeability of its types the other could not show us such a clear-cut diversity of character and manners. It is here the static definition, the completeness of every character at every moment, that points the diversity and makes it self-evident. To see sharply the difference between a multitude of living things we must arrest their movement. They must not change while we look, or the change will confuse our sense of distinction; difference will merge at times into identity, to disentangle itself and to merge again. By the same analogy, to produce a sense of diversity of character with the maximum effect, the figures must be rendered static, or rather must be seen as static, as certain types of imagination in fact see them. If all this is so, however, the limitations of the dramatic and the character novel, in appearance arbitrary, are in reality reasonable and necessary, for only by observing them can the writer get his effect and externalize his peculiar vision of life.

Franz Kafka

Kafka starts with a general or universal situation, not a particular one. This being so, it does not matter where he begins his story, for the situation is always there, and always the same. He does not have to wait, like most writers, for some incident, some human entanglement, to strike his imagination. A mere subject for a story in the ordinary sense, indeed, would cramp his powers; he would feel it as a constraint. In his diary he notes that when he tries to write on a set theme he is quite at a loss, but that as soon as he scribbles down a sentence such as 'He stood at the window and looked down at the street', he knows he is right. It is one of the quite ordinary doors through which he can enter the universal situation. Emerson says, 'The way to the centre is everywhere equally short', and Kafka might have echoed the thought in a different intonation.

As the situation is universal and stationary, it is also storyless; and this is the point at which Kafka's art begins. He is a great story-teller because there is no story for him to tell; so that he has to make it up. No foundation in fact, no narrative framework, no plot or scene for a plot is there to help him; he has to create the story, character, setting and action, and embody in it his meaning. But there a difficulty arises. For the meaning of a universal situation is inexhaustible; the story can, and actually should, go on for ever; whether it ends or not is unimportant. In his three great stories the endings are indicated, but there are gaps in the story, how great or how small it is impossible to say; and this does not matter.

His stories generally begin in the midway of life, at a point decided by the chance of the moment, and yet at a decisive point, since in the universal situation every point is decisive. The image of a road comes into our minds when we think of his stories; for in spite of all the confusions and contradictions in which he was involved he held that life was a way, not a chaos, that the right way exists and can be found by a supreme and exhausting effort, and that whatever happens every human being in fact follows some way, right or wrong. The road then is there; we may imagine beside it a wayside inn from which an anonymous figure is just emerging. He looks ahead and sees, perhaps on a distant hill, a shape which he has often seen before in his journey, but always far away, and apparently inaccessible; that shape is justice, grace, truth, final reconciliation, father, God. As he gazes at it he wonders whether he is moving towards it while it is receding from him, or flying from it while it is pursuing him. He is tormented by this question, for it is insoluble by human reasoning. He feels irresistibly drawn towards that distant shape, and yet cannot overcome his dread of it. Kafka describes in *The Castle* the struggle to reach it, and in *The Trial* the flight from it. But the hero can neither reach it nor escape it, for it is enveloped in a mystery different from the ordinary mystery of human life, and he does not know the law of that mystery. The roads leading towards it are therefore deceitful; the right turn may easily chance to be the wrong, and the wrong the right. In his greatest story Kafka tells how the hero sets out on a road which seems to be leading straight to the Castle, the dwelling-place of divinity, but how after walking for a long time he finds that though it appears to be making towards the Castle it never brings him any nearer. This or something like this happens innumerable times in his stories; it may almost be said, indeed, that nothing but this happens; though the situation conceals itself behind so many veils that the event, when it occurs, always seems novel and unique.

The frustration of the hero is an intrinsic part of Kafka's theme; and it is caused by what in theological language is known as the irreconcilability of the divine and the human law; a subtle yet immeasurable disparity. Out of this dilemma Kafka fashions his stories, or rather his story, for it is one story; he has nothing else to tell. He was confirmed in his reading of it by his study of Kierkegaard, but he must himself have made that reading independently, for his whole unhappy upbringing was behind it, and particularly, his relation to his father whom he could never reach, and from whom, until he was nearly forty, he could never escape. When as a young man, with a young man's metaphysical passion, he universalized this situation, he fashioned God in his father's image. At thirty-seven he at last made a great settlement with his father in an inordinately long, eloquent letter where, having stated his case, he went on with equal scrupulousness to state his father's. Afterwards the compulsive tie binding him to his father seems to have eased, and his conception of the universal situation became less massively pessimistic. The change can be seen in the stories which he wrote during the last few years of his life, where there is an approach to serenity. In his letter to his father he used the same method as he had employed in *The Castle* and *The Trial*; for what is so striking in them is the care he takes to state both sides of the problem: man's side, and God's.

But the supreme originality of Kafka's work does not lie in his reading of the universal position, which he shared with Kierkegaard at some points, but in his story-telling, by means of which he created a world. He is a great story-teller both by his art and by the interest and value of what he says. And the value of what he says does not depend on the truth of his metaphysical structure, any more than the value of what Dante says depends on his theology. We can read *The Castle* and *The Trial* rejecting his theory of the irreconcilability of divine and human law, and yet find in them the most enchanting discoveries, the most startling riddles, the most profound insights into human life. It is these that give his work its endless interest: the metaphysical structure, impressive as it is, is only a structure. But he enchants us equally by his art. To read him is to realize what the craft of story-telling exists for. Though modern realistic practice may conceal the fact, it is clear that story-telling is essentially a matter of invention; for all that any writer can start with is a mere narrative framework, and invention of scene and detail and dialogue alone can give it life. Kafka does not have even a narrative framework; so that the story becomes invention and nothing else. And though this may seem a drawback, it is really an advantage; for the invention, being new by necessity, is endlessly surprising, as invention should be. The scenes and figures and conversations seem to rise out of nothing, since nothing resembling them was there before. We contemplate them as we contemplate things which we see for the first time. As they exist in a world which is strange to us, the narrator has to describe them with minute exactitude; and from this necessity springs one of the most delightful graces of Kafka's art, his circumstantiality. To describe circumstantially a railway station or a large hotel or a public-house would weary us, since we are likely to know them; but Kafka's detail is more like that of a travel book which recounts minutely the customs, dresses and utensils of some newly discovered tribe; everything is strange. Besides, each detail in these stories has a purpose, and tells us something which has to be told, and is an intrinsic part of the story. Or of the structure; for *The Castle* and *The Trial* are not only stories, but edifices built according to a metaphysical specification. As the story proceeds the edifice rises.

The hero of the two great stories is anybody, and his story is the story of anybody. 'Anybody' is obviously an allegorical figure, fit to be designated as K. or Josef K., as Kafka names the heroes of *The Castle* and *The Trial*. Yet these stories are not allegories. The truths they bring out are surprising or startling, not conventional and expected, as the truths of allegory tend to be. They are more like serious fantasies; the spontaneous expression of Kafka's genius was fantasy, as his early short stories show. Fantasy came as naturally to him as writing. In *The Castle* and *The Trial* he employs it for purposes as serious as any writer has ever attempted. But no designation of his art is satisfying. We can see what it was not; to find a name for it is of little consequence.

Oswald Spengler

Oswald Spengler once had a great vogue in Germany. He first became known in England when volume one of his chief work, *The Downfall of the West* (Der Untergang des Abendlandes), was translated after the 1914–18 war. It was not so well received as in Germany: some of the reviews were adverse; but the majority were respectful or enthusiastic. Spengler's reputation in England was ruined by the translation of his last book, *Years of Decision* (Jahre der Entscheidung), in which he prophesied two centuries of world wars. It was a short book written in a popular style, and in spite of the horrifying prospect which it opened into the future, it stated explicitly the chief heads of Spengler's philosophy of history. I wish in this essay to enquire into one or two aspects of that philosophy.

I had better deal first with Spengler's verbal brutality, which, though it fits his philosophy well enough, is not necessary to it. He is fond of such generalizations as:

> Man is a *beast of prey*. I shall never tire of proclaiming that. All the moralizers and social uplifters who would pretend to be something better are only beasts of prey with their teeth drawn. When I call a man a beast of prey whom do I insult, man – or the beast? For the great beasts of prey are consummately noble creatures, and without the hypocrisy of a human morality based on weakness.

The essential thing here is Spengler's inflection, not what he says. Many people before him have held that man is a beast of prey; Hobbes did so. But he did not think it was a noble or edifying fact; he did not romantically exalt the lion, the tiger, and the shark, and exhort man to become like them. This is what Spengler does; beast of prey in his vocabulary is a term of praise; and this fact is only to be accounted for in part by his philosophy of history, and requires further explanation. The explanation, I think, is that he belongs to a special class of writer: the pseudo-man of action. Carlyle, who belonged to it too, occasionally made assertions of a similar kind, and Nietzsche did so fairly often. Real men of action do not write in this way; they can be brutal, but not romantically brutal; they know too much about the human tiger and shark. The pseudo-man of action alone romanticizes brutality in this way, and by the pseudo-man of action I do not mean the man who, but for some physical or other incidental defect, might have become a great figure in history, but the man who lives in a dream of action, imagining that by the ardour of his dream he influences events. Carlyle behaves in this way when he exhorts Cromwell at the critical point of battles, forgetting that his exhortations come two centuries too late; Nietzsche, when he constitutes himself the official midwife of a Superman who is never born; and Spengler, when he implies that in writing about history he is in some way making it. A man who is not framed for action will commit the most shocking errors in writing about it and violate the moral sense of ordinary people without being in the least conscious that he is doing so. Carlyle and Nietzsche were in practical capacity below, not above, the average; but they felt a need to identify themselves in some way with action. The result was a sort of sycophancy towards all men who could do things: the attitude of a weak boy to a strong one, or of a country doctor superintending the birth of the young master at the big house. The task of the reason is to judge action; but men like Carlyle and Nietzsche who live in a vicarious dream of action can only glorify it, betraying reason to their infatuations. Spengler does this too; but his god is not any man of action in particular, but history, which is action generalized; and as he writes of it as a pseudo-man of action, his history is really a dream of history.

A dream of history can be constructed only by a man who knows a good deal of history; and as knowledge is always respectable, such dreams are accorded a greater intellectual estimation than the dream of fair women which inspired one of Tennyson's poems. They postulate, for one thing, 'the historical sense', a modern faculty which is very useful and enjoys a great deal of prestige. The historical sense, as writers like Spengler employ it, envisages human life as a finite phenomenon completely hemmed in by Time. Time determines the forms of human life at different periods, making it a different thing, for instance, in ancient Greece from what is is to-day. Though this is a platitude it is one which in our age has acquired a new importance. But historical time is also a process with laws of its own, by virtue of which civilizations rise, grow, flourish and decay (Spengler's favourite theme) in accordance with a necessity which no human effort can influence; and human life, at any point at which we may consider it, is merely an effect of that process. Everyone who possesses the historical sense does not go to such extremes as this; but Spengler does; he makes of history, or rather of the historical process, the sole significant embodiment of human life, and consistently implies that the individual human existence is not of the slightest consequence.

The best way to show this is to allow him to speak for himself:

We live in a mighty age. It is the greatest that the culture of the West has ever seen or ever will see, the same that the ancient world knew between Cannae and Actium, the age that produced the splendid names of Hannibal, Scipio, Gracchus, Marius, Sulla, Caesar. The Great War was only the first lightning flash falling from the thunder-cloud which floats, heavy with fate, over this century. *The form of the world* is today being radically remoulded as it was by the nascent Imperium Romanum, without regarding the desires and wishes of 'the many', or counting the sacrifices which *every* such decision demands. But who can understand this? Who can endure this thought? Who can feel it a joy to be alive when this is happening? The age is a great one, but its men are correspondingly small. They can no longer endure tragedy, either on the stage or in real life . . . But the destiny which flung them into this decade has them by the throat and will do with them what must be done, whether they will or no. The cowardly safety of the end of last century is over. *Life as danger*, the *real* life of history, once more enters into its right . . . Now only the man who *dares*, who has the courage to see and deal with things as they are, really counts. A time is coming – more, it is already here! – which will have no room for sensitive souls and frail ideals. The ancient barbarism which for centuries lay fettered and buried beneath the strict forms of a high culture is awakening again, now that that culture is consummated and civilization has begun: the warlike and healthy joy in a man's own strength, which an age of rationalist thought saturated in literature despised; the unbroken instinct of race, which is resolved to live otherwise than under the oppression of piles of dead books and bookish ideals.

This is simultaneously a glorification of the Nazi creed, and an intimation that Germany need not put up with its first defeat.

Again it is the bombastic inflection that arrests the attention most loudly; Spengler is so in love with tragedy that anyone who does not welcome it with open arms, whether as torture, mutilation, sudden death, or mere starvation, is not worth his consideration. But the important thing about this passage is that it embodies his view of history, and consequently his view of human life. I shall quote one or two further passages to make this clear:

In ages of high culture human history is the history of political powers. The form of that history is war. Peace is only another variety of it. It is the continuation of war with other means . . . Domestic politics exists solely to secure the power and unity of external politics. Where it follows other aims of its own the state begins to decline . . .

A strong race must not only have an inexhaustible birthrate, but also a rigid process of selection through the hardships of life, accident, sickness and war. The medical science of the nineteenth century, a true product of rationalism, is from this point of view a sign of decadence.

This view of history and of human life is put forward quite seriously and has been accepted by many people. The two most obvious things about it are that it makes no allowance for the moral impulses of mankind, and that it grants no value to individual existence. For it, Christ is non-existent either as a historical figure or as a spiritual reality. Man as an individual exists only in so far as he furthers some change in the perpetual process of change that is called history. And history itself is merely a play of forces, in which one factor, and one factor alone, is decisive: power. This is our life in its essence: the rest is talk, morality, day-dreaming, ideology.

The best way to estimate this view of life is to compare it with one which used to be universal and is still held, I think, by the great majority of people. It accepted as the unit of its general view of human life something temporally far smaller than the units of the historical sense; it saw life as a progress from the cradle to the grave, not as the growth, fruition, decline and downfall of civilizations. It started from the individual but reached the universal, since individuality is the universal form in which human life manifests itself. Accepting individuality as the norm, it sought to discover the nature of the laws which govern the individual existence, and its ultimate meaning. This was a task which carried it beyond history into religion; for the view of life of which I am speaking could not admit that human life was a historical phenomenon and nothing more. Mankind's secular destiny was certainly worked out in history, and history was therefore a process of the utmost significance. But man was also an immortal soul, whose essence could never be seized and contained by history. He had longings which history could not satisfy, and sorrows of which history took no account. He was an actor simultaneously in the historical drama and in another whose terms were strange to history: a drama of sin and atonement, aspiration and failure, which implied a responsibility to something beyond time. On this foundation the old traditional view of human life was based: on man's existence from birth to death, and on immortality. It took into account not only what man succeeded in being on this earth (that is history), but all that he failed to be. History is the record of human limitation; it accepts action effectively operative in time, and nothing more. Religion accepts the totality of human desire, disappointment and fulfilment, whether effectively operative in time or not. Its basis is therefore wider than that of history, though temporally it seems more restricted: the life of a human being from birth to death. Accordingly it could not dismiss morality and individuality as mere trimmings of existence, and assume, as Spengler does, that they are of no importance. It accepted them as essential attributes of human nature, and tried to account for them and give them a meaning.

Now it seems to me that we are seeing to-day a fight between these two views of life: the religious view, which is also that of the artist, and the historical view. The virtue of the first – not its supreme virtue, which is its truth, but its relative pragmatic virtue – is that it gives meaning to the actual life we live, and accounts to us for ourselves. In one of his essays Alexander Blok, the Russian poet, claimed that the time of 'Goodness, Beauty and Truth' was past. That is a typical if extreme utterance of the historical sense, and at the same time an error which could have been avoided by remembering that human life is a life between birth and death, and that in that life the individual, whether civilized or savage, cannot but have some relation, positive or negative, to Goodness, Beauty and Truth. Spengler, politically a bitter enemy of everything Blok believed in, thought here in the same way. To him the one operative factor in existence is not goodness, beauty or truth, but power, and so he praises the beast of prey and pours scorn on 'a human morality based on weakness'. The old view of life sees endless variety and complexity in human existence, and yet makes certain fundamental distinctions: good and evil, truth and falsehood, guilt and innocence. The new historical view as expressed by Spengler sees no essential variety in human existence at all, but only the category of power, or, in other words, of necessity; and yet, in spite of its simplicity, it leads to no conclusion: it remains on the plane of pure relativity. And on the plane of pure relativity it is possible to prefer anything to anything else: a well-grown tiger to Socrates or Christ, brutality to kindness, cunning to honesty, treachery to good faith. One can therefore say with a good conscience: 'The medical science of the nineteenth century, a true product of rationalism, is . . . a sign of decadence', or: 'Few can stand a long war. But nobody could stand a long peace', because one has no palpable human reality to hold on to, and has forgotten the pitiful limitations and the necessary virtues of existence as the individual knows it. So in men without imagination, like Spengler, the spectacle of history can easily rouse an irrational arrogance. The historian who accepts the limitations of ordinary existence may find some matter for grief in contemplating battlefields and massacres; but the feelings of a man who regards history as the sole meaning of human life must be somewhat different, and it may easily be beneath him to 'regard the desires and wishes' or 'count the sacrifices' of 'the many'. And here we come to the point where Spengler's verbal brutality and his philosophy of history meet. A purely relative view of human destiny based on a theory of a play of forces gives an opportunity, indeed a justification, for brutality.

Another danger of a view of life which is not based on the fundamental fact of the individual human existence is that it is extremely susceptible to fashion. The history of Spengler's literary development is instructive. In 1918 Germany was defeated, and a few years later there appeared the first volume of *The Downfall of the West*, proclaiming that all Europe was doomed. After the peace came the German inflation, one of whose effects was that the German peasantry hoarded their produce or profiteered in it, so that a lively antipathy arose between the country and the towns. Presently appeared the second volume of *The Downfall of the West* which prophesied, among other things, that one of the decisive struggles of the future would be the struggle between the country and the towns. But meanwhile Germany had become a tepidly Social Democratic Republic, and Spengler published another book called *Prussianism and Socialism*, in which he tried to show that both political forms were inspired by the same ideal. Then German Social Democracy entered into its swift decline, and with the advent of Hitler Spengler's last book, *Years of Decision*, appeared, which foretold the rise of a whole line of Caesars.

By all this I do not intend to cast any aspersion on Spengler's honesty, but merely to show that he was a man extremely susceptible to fashion. He was obviously sincere when he complained, in a footnote to his last book, that 'What I described in *Prussianism and Socialism* – and it has almost always been misunderstood – was Socialism *as an ethical attitude,* not as a materialistic economic principle'. Fashion is a sweeping generalization from insufficient or trivial evidence; and that might be a description of all Spengler's books. The temporary downfall of Germany after the war, enlarged and touched up in his dream of history, became the final downfall of Europe. The appearance of Hitler was sufficient to presume the advent of a whole line of Caesars. A few years were sufficient to change Spengler's conclusions about the whole future of history. Yet these conclusions were formulated as universal truths; facts as incontestable as the latest mode. And this is understandable, for the historical sense must always be revising its conception of history in accordance with the contemporary growth of history. It has no hold on any other reality. And without a hold on some other reality, it is impossible to have a true conception of human existence.

Spengler was an excellent pamphleteer with an astonishing gift for facile generalization; he was not, as a thinker, of any importance. But he was of some importance as a wholesale dealer in the historical sense, as a man who employed the historical sense with unexampled irresponsibility, so that in his works it can see a caricature of itself. The historical sense is a useful method for viewing human life in the large; but when it edges out every other method, invading not only history, where it is only partially valid, but fiction and poetry as well, it becomes a great danger.

Poetry and the Poet

I want to say a few things about poetry, the forms in which it is embodied and the spirit which animates these forms. The forms range from the simple folk song and ballad to the poetic comedy and tragedy and the epic. Regarding poetry in its extent, we find there an extraordinary variety of forms and discover that they all have a purpose and a wonderful suitability. Looking back over the history of poetry, we see that endless invention and modification have gone into these forms, from the small compact sonnet to blank verse, the greatest innovation in English poetry. All these forms have an organic function, which is lacking in free verse. In our own time free verse has had a very considerable influence, which now seems to be passing. The main defect of free verse is monotony; it can be used apparently for any subject and any mood; there is no escape for the writer of free verse except into free verse. The whole world of forms, the whole variety of poetic expression, lies outside. The poet, it seems to me, attains his freedom through some given form or set of forms. There may well be new forms still to come, for language changes and may bring about the use of other rhythmical measures.

These metrical forms are subject to the accidents of time; they fall into disuse in ages when they are found to be unsuitable for the expression of contemporary feeling, and may later be revived when they become employable again. Through them poetry speaks to us not only in the speech of our time and out of the world we know, but from past ages, since they have existed for a long time, and connect the present with the past. The problem of communication is often discussed by poets and critics. In writing a poem should the poet have the conscious intention of communicating with his readers? This is a difficult question. Perhaps the intention to communicate is always there, though the poet may not be conscious of it. Yet, if he is to communicate something of value, his attention must obviously remain fixed on the poem. For it is the poem that communicates with us; and it does this, in great poetry, long after the poet's death. Perhaps this is because poetry is itself the communication of something for which no other kind of speech can serve; it is certainly not because the poet sets out with the idea that he must communicate. The discussions of contemporary poetry are beset with false problems. The more perfectly achieved a poem is, the more fully it will be apprehended by those who read it. Deliberate intention, anything which distracts the poet from what he seeks to express, may become an obstacle to understanding. A folk song that sings for its own pleasure will give back to us for centuries the emotion out of which it was born. And a story which is thinking of nothing but the story will move us most when we forgot or do not know who is telling it.

The poetic story and the song move us partly because they are rhythmical and musical; but the rhythm and music would be extraneous and meaningless if they were not animated by imagination. By imagination I mean nothing so metaphysically hard to understand as Coleridge's definition of it, but rather a faculty which belongs to us all, in however fragmentary a degree. If we did not possess imagination in this sense, we would not be able to understand our neighbour and our friends even as imperfectly as we do, and life would be a blank for us: we would have no image of it. We would not be able even to gossip about our neighbours. Indeed, gossip is for many people the main form that imagination takes; for it involves invention and with that some rudimentary conception of life; at its common level it is a perpetual reminder that common men are subject to the same pleasures and griefs and the same absurd chances as the great. To make us feel the grief of Priam and Hecuba over the death of Hector, dead thirty centuries ago, is another thing, and far beyond the reach of gossip, yet it is not altogether different in kind. It is a high feat of imagination, and we could not respond to it if we were quite devoid of imagination ourselves.

By imagination I mean that power by which we apprehend living beings and living creatures in their individuality, as they live and move, and not as ideas or categories. The knowledge which it gives of Priam and Hecuba is of a different kind from that which history and archaeology can provide. It takes us into the feelings and thoughts of these legendary figures, and makes us feel the full weight and the uniqueness of their lives. It is as important as anything can be that we should be able to do this, for it makes us understand human life vividly and intimately in ourselves because we have felt it in others. Imagination gives us this knowledge of people and Nature, but never exact knowledge, since it cannot and does not wish to study them under the fixed conditions which make possible the exact knowledge of the scientist. The life and movement and individuality of human beings, and of beasts and birds and trees, their feelings and moods and mischances, are everything to it. Compared with science its scope is vague and incommensurable, since it embraces all possibilities of experience. Consequently, it is for human living that imagination is indispensable. Exact knowledge is only a fragment of the knowledge we need in order to live. We can have no exact knowledge of ourselves, far less of other people. There is no exact answer to the problems we are perpetually troubled by and have never solved; yet we must have some faculty by which we can deal with them. We cannot ask science to tell us whether our lives have a meaning, or why we should pursue good and avoid evil, or how we should live with our neighbours. Imagination does not answer these questions; perhaps the only answer for them is in faith. What imagination does is to give us a vivid sense of them. Such questions obstinately haunt us, and our lives would become barbarous if they ceased; we should not know or be ourselves in any human sense; we should become semi-abstractions, categories, somewhat like the figures described in George Orwell's book *1984*.

I have used the word imagination in a way which may seem to restrict it to poetry and imaginative literature, and to deny it to the scientist. That of course would be ridiculous. Perhaps the greatest intensity of imagination during the last hundred years, as well as the most intense intellectual passion, has gone into pure science. But the subjects which excite the imagination of the scientist, no matter in what branch of study, are different from those that move the imagination of the poet, and if I were to use the word in this extended sense I could not apply it with much relevance to the kind of knowledge, inexact yet essential for us, which is had by seeing into the life of things. That kind of imagination obviously had a greater sway in the earlier stages of civilization than it has now. Even less than four hundred years ago, in the Elizabethan age, poets exercised it more freely than we apparently can at present. Poetry, one might say, came more easily then to the writer than prose, and comedy and tragedy fell naturally into poetry, while, now that prose has become a broad river and poetry has dwindled into a narrow trickle, we have to use the most elaborate expedients to bring the poetic play back again. In Elizabeth's time prose itself was more suited for imagination than for thought. The great change, as we know, began in the seventeenth century and was carried to triumph in the age of reason; prose became the instrument of clear thought, and poetry for a time was forced to emulate it, so strong was the general tendency and the genuine need. Feeling and imagination were reinstated by the romantic poets, but the romantic impulse died in less than a hundred years; poetry faded into an echo in William Morris, and prose became the supreme form, universally acknowledged.

A process such as this, so imperious that it has changed the language in which we feel and think, must have had an influence, in countless ways, on our feelings and thoughts and our conception of human life. Its influence on poetry, though important enough, may be of less concern than its influence on these other things. Poetry has no quarrel with pure science, with the disinterested inquiry into the nature of things; for poetry is concerned in a different way with the same inquiry. But, if you have two great powers, both of them serviceable to human life, and one of them develops at a great speed while the other marks time, the result is bound to be dangerous. I can make only a speculative guess here. During the past three centuries, slowly at first, then more and more rapidly, the balance between the poetic imagination and the scientific intellect has been lost. Let us assume that this process began when people realized that by carefully observing and studying nature they might win mastery over it. Philosophers and scientists began to look forward to the acquisition of power over nature, yet what they had in mind was not pure but applied science, capable of creating a world such as ours but not to make us free. The thought that nature could be mastered evoked a great hope for the future of mankind, and when a hope is thrown open our energies irresistibly rush toward it. At the beginning this hope was cherished by philosophers only; but in due course it became the general hope of the Western world. A romanticism of science arose in the eighteenth century, and became almost universal in the nineteenth, the age of progress. People believed that science would work a vast transmutation on society, and bring in a sort of millennium. To measure the strength of that faith, one has only to read Macaulay's prophecy of the coming future, when universal prosperity and freedom would be the rule, and flourishing fields would cover the sides of Ben Nevis. Scientists as recent as Pasteur and Pavlov have believed in it. Few of us, whether scientists or laymen, believe in it now. We have learned that what the nineteenth century called progress has brought us where we are, and that, whenever the idea of progress is canvassed, something is left out of account. The dream of science has been justified in many ways. It has brought countless improvements in our daily life; without the dream our life would be much poorer. If the world created by science seems to us sometimes to have advanced too quickly and too far, while we have remained marking time on the same spot, that can be borne for the sake of the good that may come of it. If we feel sometimes that we are living in a future which does not fit us, that too can be borne. What imposes a greater strain on us, the real strain of modern life, is the sense, not of too much happening too quickly, but of something lacking. Something in the apparent progression has not progressed; for myself I would call it the imagination which would have made us able to use for purely human purposes all that applied science offers us. A lopsided development, whether of the body or the mind, is a diseased development, and is bound to lead to strange and unpredictable results. One of these is that people in general are troubled now by the thought of applied science, in spite of the benefits it has brought, increasing our wealth, lengthening our lives, and alleviating pain. The catalogue is endless. What we are troubled by is the sense that science has run on far ahead of us, and that we are without the wisdom to use for our good the enormous power which it drops in passing into our hands. As we do not know how to use that power, it becomes an ambiguous gift, an explosive possiblity. This is the focus of the apprehension that fills the living world, and the subject that generally comes up when people gather together.

What do people mean, loosely, when they say that science has become a danger? They obviously mean applied science and the power over things and human beings which is made possible by it. They are daunted by the world that applied science and centralized organization have built around them; they are alarmed by the thought of a future in which these powers will become irresistible and inescapable. From this arise those occasional nightmares which seem to warn us that the ordinary human being may not be able to survive, together with the traditional beliefs and customs and feelings which have fostered him and made him what he is. You will find this nightmare described in the forlorn Utopias of Aldous Huxley and George Orwell, which prophesy the end of mankind and its supersession by a species indistinguishable from it in outward appearance, but without love, goodness, and evil, or even hatred, as we have come to know them during our lives and the history of civilization. Our imaginations, when they have nothing better to do, project these vast, distorted nightmares into the future. I think we all make these projections, for in states of apprehension or foreboding we live more in the future than in the present, and are troubled by both.

What can the imagination do with this world? Something different, surely, from the manufacture of the nightmare. Hugo von Hofmannsthal said once that true imagination is always conservative. By this he may have meant that it keeps intact the bond which unites us with the past of mankind, so that we can still understand Odysseus and Penelope, and the people of the Old Testament. Or he may have meant something more: that imagination is able to do this because it sees the life of everyone as the endless repetition of a single pattern. It is hard to explain how we can enter into past lives if this is not so. We become human by repetition; in the imagination that repetition becomes an object of delighted contemplation, with all that is good and evil in it, so that we can almost understand the saying that Hector died and Troy fell that they might turn into a song. The difference between the world of imagination and the world of applied science, in which we actually spend our lives, is so great that the one can hardly understand the other. Applied science shows us a world of consistent, mechanical progress. There machines give birth to ever new generations of machines; but the point to be observed is that the new machines are always an improvement on the old, and begin where the old left off. If we attribute sentience to the new machine, we shall find that it simply does not understand the old; it is far ahead, in another world. But in the world of imagination and of human beings all is different. There you find no consistent progress, no starting where the previous generation left off; instead there is continuity. Every human being begins at the beginning, as his fathers did, with the same difficulties and pleasures, the same temptations, the same problem of good and evil, the same inward conflict, the same need to learn how to live, the same need to ask what life means. Conspicuous virtue, when he encounters it, may move him, or a new and saving faith; since the desire for goodness and truth is also in his nature. He will pass through the ancestral pattern, from birth to childhood and youth and manhood and age and death. He will feel hope and fear and love and hate and perhaps forgiveness. All this may seem dull and monotonous to the detached thinker, but it enchants the imagination for it is the image of all human life. But when change becomes too rapid, and the world around us alters from year to year, the ancestral image grows more indistinct than it was in simpler times, and the imagination cannot pierce to it as easily as it once could.

There has been change, of course, since the beginning of things.

There have been crises and revolutions in the slow development of civilization in the past. Certain generations then probably found it hard to adapt themselves to some new invention, such as the use of iron instead of stone, or the discovery of agriculture fixing the nomad to one place, or the construction of great cities, or the consolidation of elaborate states, bringing new and difficult laws. But the change was different from change as we know it in our time, both in its speed and in its nature. It was brought about by a sort of rule of thumb, as when some farmer, having watched the behaviour of nature, assisted it by planting seed in the uncovered soil; after that it was only a long step to the mattock and the plough. These changes soon appeared natural to the ordinary man and were absorbed into his life. But the great changes in modern life have been produced by means which the ordinary man does not understand. The modern workman does not know his world as the ploughman once did; sometimes he does not even understand what his hands are doing. There is a gap between him and the world which his work perpetuates, between the workman and the man himself, so that it is not easy for imagination to see through the one to the other.

This is one of the reasons why some poets are so concerned with the problem of being contemporary; they feel that the world in which they live is unlike any other with which poetry has ever dealt. The problem is a real one, and the best statement of it I know of is in an essay by Stephen Spender called 'Inside the Cage' in his critical volume, *The Making of a Poem*. Being in the cage really means being enclosed in the contemporary world, without any outlet except into a future very like but worse than the present. The cage exists, and we live in it. Yet the imagination does not live entirely in it, but in thirty centuries at least, and beyond them in the ever deepening past which archaeology is excavating. We are here, and Homer and his lost ancestors are far away. Yet on the other hand we are human beings like the men and women in Homer. We are bound to the past generations by the same bond as to our neighbours, and if only for the sake of preserving the identity of mankind we must cherish memory. This means that how we regard the past is very important.

Mr Spender, speaking of the kind of analysis which interprets the past and its works in terms of the present, says:

The dead and their works should be regarded not as illustrations of the ideology of the living but as coherent indissoluble unities situated in past time. The sun and moon, like Dante and Shakespeare, are far removed in time when their light reaches us, but we do not, for that reason, consider that the principles according to which they exist are 'historically correct for their time', though not for ours ... The organised realities in Dante and Shakespeare do not lead up to our contemporary development, they look at it and criticise it. All co-exist. But in order to understand this we have to see the reality of the dead as in some way absolute in itself, and impossible to dissolve into our ideas unless we are to be imprisoned in our own present. To talk about 'the suspension of disbelief' in approaching the faiths of the past, already betrays the analytic attitude which attempts to convert past beliefs into *our* ideas, and then finds them unacceptable. We have to accept that past belief was a fact, like a rock. And probably what is required of us today is something far more complex than the so-called complexities of analysis; we need both to employ the analytic method and to reject it. To analyse the work, and to realise at the same time that it maintains its own intrinsic reality, like sun and moon, outside the analysis. What matters is contact with the dead and their works as existent – coexistent – fact, outside any attempt to resolve them into our ideas.

Mr Spender, I think, has the Marxian theory in mind in what he says, and, perhaps, though it is so far removed from Marx, the new criticism as well. He says of the one: 'No system which insists on analysing all pasts and presents outside itself into its own ideology can co-exist with any other present or past.' And he goes on: 'However, even without Marxism, the co-existence which is talked of so glibly today, is in fact almost an unattainable ideal. Through the excessive practice of analytic methods and the widespread belief that analysis of the fact is more significant than the fact itself, every country, every culture, every school of thought has become isolated within its own terms.'

The past is a living past, and past and present coexist: that also the imagination tells us. It opens the past to us as part of our own life, a vast extension of our present. It cannot admit that anything that ever happened among the dead is dead for us, or that all that men and women have done and suffered was merely meant to bring us where we are.

Yet, in spite of all that the past means for us, and although it remains so obstinately alive in the imagination, the remedy is not to keep living in it and turn away from the present. The acceptance of the past can enlarge and purify our image of human life; and Dante and Shakespeare do look at and criticize our age. But they did not know our age; they only knew something that is true of life in any age. Our contemporary life also asks to be interpreted in poetry, and, because it is so unlike that of any former age, has a peculiar need for those who can imaginatively interpret it. I have said a great deal about the present difficulties of poetry, and have tried to explain some of them, hoping that explanation may be of some use. I have spoken of the enigma of the public, and the ascendency of criticism, and science, and the effect on the imagination of a world becoming more and more a world of secondary objects. I have also tried to give an idea of the virtue of the poetic imagination, its ancient succession, and the urgent need for it in our time. Poetry in any age is bound to be contemporary. What I have tried to urge is that poetry will not truly be contemporary, or truly poetry, if it deals merely with the immediately perceived contemporary world as if that existed by itself and were isolated from all that preceded it. As it is, our age offers opportunities for the imagination as well as difficulties: anthropology and archaeology have extended the possible world of imagination in time, while psychology has explored the regions of the unconscious. It is the contemporary world itself which presents us with these new provinces accessible to the imagination, and the poet is free to use them for his own purposes, though he will not, of course, use them in the same way as the archaeologist and the psychologist. The categories of psychology will probably be of little use to him, and may do him harm; but the dream life of the unconscious with his own image of life is certain some time to enter into and deepen the archetypal images of the imagination. I mean the actual dream life, not the daydream or the decorative fantasy. There is this vast background of existence only guessed at in past poetry at moments when it did not quite know what it was doing. Perhaps in that obscure region we still exist timelessly, though we may be lying asleep in a modern bed in the modern world.

The relation between time past, time present, and time future is always with us, and we are reminded of it in T. S. Eliot's poem 'Four Quartets'. Our world presents the imagination with certain questions not asked before, or not asked in the same way. Public indifference may be expected to continue, but perhaps the audience will increase when poetry loses what obscurity is left in it by attempting greater themes, for great themes have to be stated clearly. A great theme greatly treated might still put poetry back in its old place.

AUTOBIOGRAPHY
AND TRAVEL

Wyre

I was born on 15th May, 1887, in a farm called the Folly, in the parish of Deerness in Orkney. My father left it when I was two, so that I have no early memories of it, and as the house has since been pulled down and the farm joined to another farm, all that I know of it are the foundations, which I was shown a few years ago: a long, narrow house looking down towards the sea and the isle of Copinsay over a sloping field.

My father came from the island of Sanday, which is filled with Muirs and Sinclairs, families who came over from Caithness after the Stewarts at the beginning of the sixteenth century. I can follow my own branch no further back than my father's father, who had a farm in Sanday called Colligarth. My mother's name was Elizabeth Cormack, and my knowledge of her family again goes back only to her father, Edwin Cormack, after whom I was named. There is in Deerness a ruined chapel which was built in the eighth or ninth century by an Irish priest called Cormack the Sailor, who was later canonized; it is only a few miles from Haco, the farm where my mother was born. Whether the names are connected over the great stretch of time in that small corner no one can say; but it is conceivable, for in Orkney families have lived in the same place for many hundreds of years, and I like to think that some people in the parish, myself among them, may have a saint among their ancestors, since some of the Irish priests were not celibate.

My mother lived much more in the past than my father, so that when I was a child Deerness became a lively place to me, while Sanday remained blank except for its witches, since the tales my father told me were mainly about the supernatural. One of my mother's stories has stuck in my memory. The family had moved from Haco to Skaill, a farm on the edge of a sandy bay, beside the

77

parish church and the churchyard. She was eighteen at the time. The rest of the family had gone up to the Free Kirk, two miles away, for an evening prayer meeting, a great revival having swept the islands. It was a wild night of wind and sleet, and she was sitting in the kitchen reading, when the door opened and ten tall men, dripping with water, came in and sat round the fire. They spoke to her, but she could not tell what they were saying. She sat on in a corner, dumb with terror, until the family came back two hours later. The men were Danes, and their ship had split on a rock at the end of the bay.

Both her memory and my father's were filled with wrecks, for the Orkney coast is dangerous, and at that time there were few light-houses. When the wrecks were washed ashore the people in the parish gathered and took their pick. Stories were told of men luring ships on to the rocks by leading a pony along a steep road with a green light tied to one side and a red light to the other. It was said, too, that ministers sometimes prayed for a wreck in bad times. A strange tale often told in our family is indirectly connected with all this. One bright moonlight night my father and my cousin Sutherland were standing at the end of the house at the Folly after feeding the cattle, when they saw a great three-masted vessel making straight for the shore. They watched in amazement for a few minutes – there was only a field between them and it – until it melted into a black mist on the water. I was enchanted by this story when I heard it, but as I grew older I naturally began to doubt it. Then when I was seventeen or eighteen I was speaking to a farmer who had lived on the neighbour-ing farm of the Barns, and he told me the very same story. He had been at the end of his house that night, and he too had seen the three-master standing in for the shore and then disappearing. At the time he was amazed at its behaviour, like my father and my cousin Sutherland, for in the bright moonlight the cliffs must have been clearly visible from the ship; but they all accepted it, I think, as a magical occurrence.

My father's stories were drawn mostly from an earlier age, and I think must have been handed on to him by his own father. They went back to the Napoleonic wars, the press-gang, and keelhauling, which still left a memory of terror in Orkney. But in his own time he had known several witches, who had 'taken the profit of the corn', turned the milk sour, and wrecked ships by raising storms. Many of these stories I have heard since in other versions, and these obviously come from the store of legends that gathered when witch-burning was common in Scotland. In one a Sanday farmer, coming back for his dinner, saw the local witch's black cat slinking out of his house. He rushed in, snatched up his gun, and let fly at it. The cat was leaping over a stone dyke when he fired; it stumbled and gave a great screech, then ran away, dragging one hind-leg after it. Next day the witch sent for the doctor to set her leg. My father told this story so well that I could see the farmer with the smoking gun in his hands, and the black cat stumbling over the grey stone wall and running away with a twisted, crablike glide. When my father told his witch stories we sat up very late; we were afraid to go to bed.

The devil himself, as Auld Nick, sometimes came into these tales, and generally in the same way. A farmer would be in the barn threshing his corn with a flail, when he would notice another flail keeping time with him, and looking up would see an enormous, naked, coal-black man with a fine upcurling tail standing opposite him. He fainted at this point, and when he awoke all the corn in the barn would be neatly threshed. But these visits were always followed by bad luck.

My father had also a great number of stories about the Book of Black Arts. This book could be bought only for a silver coin, and sold only for a smaller silver one. It ended in the possession of a foolish servant-girl who paid a threepenny-piece for it. It was very valuable, for it gave you all sorts of worldly power; but it had the drawback that if you could not sell it to some one before you died you would be damned. The servant-girl of my father's story tried every means to get rid of it. She tore it to pieces, buried it, tied a stone to it and flung it into the sea, burned it; but after all this it was still at the bottom of her chest when she went to look there. What happened in the end I can't remember; I fancy the poor girl went off her head. I always thought of the book as a great, black, hasped, leather-bound volume somewhat like a family Bible.

My father also knew the horseman's word – that is, the word which will make a horse do anything you desire if you whisper it into its ear. Some time ago I asked Eric Linklater, who knows Orkney now better than I do, if he had ever heard of the horseman's word up there. He said no, but he told me that when he was a student at Aberdeen University young ploughmen in Buchan were willing to pay anything from ten shillings to a pound out of their small wages to be told the horseman's word. From what my father said I imagine that the word was a shocking one.

The Orkney I was born into was a place where there was no great distinction between the ordinary and the fabulous; the lives of living men turned into legend. A man I knew once sailed out in a boat to look for a mermaid, and claimed afterwards that he had talked with her. Fantastic feats of strength were commonly reported. Fairies, or 'fairicks', as they were called, were encountered dancing on the sands on moonlight nights. From people's talk they were small, graceful creatures about the size of leprechauns, but pretty, not grotesque. There was no harm in them. All these things have vanished from Orkney in the last fifty years under the pressure of compulsory education.

My father left the Folly for a farm called the Bu in the island of Wyre. There were seven other farms on the island, with names which went back to the viking times: Russness, Onziebist, Helzigartha, Caivit, Testaquoy, Habreck, the Haa. The Bu was the biggest farm in the island, and close beside a little green knoll called the Castle. In the eleventh century this had been the stronghold of a viking freebooter called Kolbein Hruga, or Cubby Roo, but we did not know this at the time, nor did any of our neighbours: all that remained was the name and the knoll and a little cairn of big stones. Between the house and the knoll there was a damp green meadow which waved with wild cotton in summer. Then came the dry, smooth slope of the Castle, and on the top the round cairn of square grey stones, as high as a man's shoulder and easy for us to climb. My younger sister and I would sit there for hours in the summer evenings, looking across the sound at the dark, hilly island of Rousay, which also had its castle, a brand-new one like a polished black-and-white dice, where a retired general lived: our landlord. He was a stylish, very little man with a dapper walk, and the story went that because of his size he had been the first to pass through the breach in the wall of Lucknow when that town was relieved during the Indian Mutiny. He came over to Wyre every spring to shoot the wild birds. I remember one soft spring day when the light seemed to be opening up the world after the dark winter; I must have been five at the time, for it was before I went to school. I was standing at the end of the house; I think I had just recovered from some illness, and everything looked clean and new. The General was walking through the field below our house in his little brown jacket with the brown leather tabs on the shoulders, his neat little knickerbockers and elegant little brown boots; a feather curled on his hat, and his little pointed beard seemed to curl too. Now and then he raised his silver gun, the white smoke curled upward, birds fell, suddenly heavy after seeming so light; our cattle, who were grazing in the field, rushed away in alarm at the noise, then stopped and looked round in wonder at the strange little man. It was a mere picture; I did not feel angry with the General or sorry for the birds; I was entranced with the bright gun, the white smoke, and particularly with the soft brown tabs of leather on the shoulders of his jacket. My mother was standing at the end of the house with me; the General came over and spoke to her, then, calling me to him, gave me a sixpence. My father appeared from some-where, but replied very distantly to the General's affable words. He was a bad landlord, and in a few years drove my father out of the farm by his exactions.

Between our house and the school there was a small, roofless chapel which had once been the chapel of the Castle. In summer it was a jungle of nettles and rank weeds, which on hot days gave out a burning smell that scorched my nostrils. At the school, which stood on a slight rising, a new group of more distant islands appeared, some of them brown, some green with light sandy patches. Not a tree anywhere. There were only two things that rose from these low, rounded islands: a high, top-heavy castle in Shapinsay, standing by itself with the insane look of tall, narrow houses in flat, wide landscapes, and in Egilsay a black chapel with a round, pointed tower, where St Magnus had been murdered in the twelfth century. It was the most beautiful thing within sight, and it rose every day against the sky until it seemed to become a sign in the fable of our lives.

Besides my father and mother and my three brothers and two sisters there were two other members of our household: my aunt Maggie and my cousin Sutherland. Maggie was an elder, unmarried sister of my father. She had a perfectly grey face, the colour of peat ash, a well-shaped nose a size too large for it, a mouth like a handsome young man's, and clear, almost colourless eyes. She always wore a napkin round her head, tied so as to form a little penthouse over her brow, so that looked at from the side she seemed to have two noses of the same shape and size, one above the other. She was a small woman, but had a long loping stride which made her look as if she were always running. Like most old people in Orkney at that time, she was bothered with all sorts of ailments – rheumatics in the joints, wind, pains at the pit of the stomach; and she always kept in her own room what she called a 'phial', her fond diminutive for 'bottle', though whether it contained medicine or alcohol we were never sure. She used snuff, and drank a great quantity of baking-soda with water. I think she must have been a bitter, disappointed woman, for she was always talking of the lovers she had rejected as a young girl. But to us she was merely odd, and we teased her a great deal, especially after we caught her one night trying to get rid of a wart on her finger by pointing a straw first at it and then at the moon, and muttering something to herself.

My cousin Sutherland was the most original character in the house. I remember him as a little man in a blue jersey and trousers with a dashing fall. His body swung forward from his hips, as if he were always on the point of offering something with his hands. His head was like a battering-ram, and dusty brown hair like an animal's fell stood stiffly up from it. His sparkling grey eyes were nautical, his bulbous nose ecclesiastical, his bushy brown moustache military. Before he made a joke he would pass the back of his hand under his moustache with a casual succulent sweep which left his arm neg- ligently hanging in the air, as if he had forgotten it for the moment but would presently remember it again. All his movements melted into each other with the continuity of a tree. His skin was reptilian; his head sloped, like a tortoise's, into his neck, his shoulders into his trunk. He was very strong and crafty, and in wrestling could bring down men much younger and heavier than himself. His ordinary stance then was a lazy crouch; he would roll waggishly on his feet, as if he were keeping his balance in a slight swell; he was very light-footed. His appearance never changed while I knew him; he looked thirty-five all the time.

Sutherland had more natural slyness of a harmless kind than any man I have ever known. Since he was lecherous as well he was a great danger to the young women of Wyre, Rousay, and Egilsay; for on calm summer nights he would sail to these other islands with a boatload of young men and try his fortune with the strange women. I fancy he never attempted to display himself to them in a romantic light, for when he wanted a favour he always referred to himself as 'Old Sutherland' in an objective yet cajoling way. His language was very free, and his advances shockingly direct, but always with a show of reason. He never tried to show the women why they should yield to him, but concentrated on the much more subtle question 'Why not?' a question very difficult to answer. He was the father of a number of illegitimate children, and I remember my father once saying in a vexed voice, 'Why, the man canna look at a woman, it seems, withoot putting her in the family way!' I was too young at the time to understand these words.

Whenever Sutherland got drunk he began to invent language. I can't remember now many of his feats in this way, but he liked words with a dashing Spanish sound, like 'yickahooka' and 'navahonta.' He was so pleased with the word 'tramcollicken', which he invented himself, that he gave it a specific meaning which I had better not mention; but the word became so popular that it spread all over Wyre. From somewhere or other he had picked up 'graminivorous', which struck him by its comic sound, and for a long time his usual greeting was, 'Weel, boy, how's thee graminivorous tramcollicken?' Macedonia, Arabia, Valparaiso, and Balaclava became parts of his ordinary vocabulary, giving him a sense of style and grandeur. He was a great singer at concerts, or *soirées*, as he always called them, and gave dashing renderings of 'Poor blind Joe' and 'When Jack comes home again'. On Sunday afternoons he sat on the kitchen bed snuffling the Psalms with his face sanctimoniously lengthened. But in the evening he set out for some neighbouring farm to see what he could get out of the women.

My first definite memories are connected with the Bu; but there is one composite one which may conceivably go back to the house where I was born, it brings such a sense of timelessness with it. I was lying in some room watching a beam of slanting light in which dusty, bright motes slowly danced and turned, while a low murmuring went on somewhere, possibly the humming of flies. My mother was in the room, but where I do not know; I was merely conscious of her as a vague, environing presence. This picture is clear and yet indefinite, attached to one summer day at the Bu, and at the same time to so many others that it may go back to the day when I first watched a beam of light as I lay in my cradle. The quiet murmuring, the slow, unending dance of the motes, the sense of deep and solid peace, have come back to me since only in dreams. This memory has a different quality from any other memory in my life. It was as if, while I lay watching that beam of light, time had not yet begun.

My first definite memory is of being baptized. Why I was not baptized in Deerness, where there were two churches, I have never been able to find out; but the ceremony was postponed for some reason until I was three years old. I was dressed for the occasion in a scarlet suit with petticoats instead of breeches, for boys were not given boys' clothes then until they were five. The suit was made of some fine but slightly rough material like serge; the sun must have been shining that day, for the cloth seemed to glow from within with its own light; it was fastened with large glittering golden buttons. I think it must have been the first time that I saw the colour of gold and of scarlet, for it is this suit that makes me remember that day, and it still burns in my memory more brightly than anything I have ever seen since. In the afternoon my father and mother led me by the hand to the school, where Mr Pirie, the minister of Rousay, had come to baptize me. Some people had gathered. I was lifted up by my father, face upward; I saw Mr Pirie's kind face with its thin beard inclined diagonally over me (for he had a glass eye and looked at everything from the side), then I felt the cold water on my face and began to cry. As if the baptismal water had been a deluge, all the rest of that day is damp and drowned, the burning scarlet and the gold sunk in darkness.

I can see the rough grey stones spotted with lichen on the top of the Castle, and a bedraggled gooseberry bush in a corner of the garden whose branches I lovingly fingered for hours; but I cannot bring back the feelings which I had for them, the sense of being magically close to them, as if they were magnets drawing me with a palpable power. Reasonable explanations can be found for these feelings: the fact that every object is new to a child, that he sees it without understanding it, or understands it with a different understanding from that of experience – different, for there may be fear in it, but there cannot be calculation or worry; or even the fact that he is closer to things, since his eyes are only two or three feet from the ground, not five or six. Grass, stones, and insects are twice as near to him as they will be after he has grown up, and when I try to re-create my early childhood it seems to me that it was focused on such things as these, and that I lived my life in a small, separate underworld, while the grown-ups walked on their long legs several feet above my head on a stage where every relation was different. I was dizzily lifted into that world, as into another dimension, when my father took me on his shoulders, so that I could see the roof of the byre from above or touch the lintel of the house door with my hand. But for most of the time I lived with whatever I found on the surface of the earth: the different kinds of grass, the daisies, buttercups, dandelions, bog cotton (we did not have many flowers), the stones and bits of glass and china, and the scurrying insects which made my stomach heave as I stared at them, unable to take my eyes away. These insects were all characters to me, interesting but squalid, with thoughts that could never be penetrated, inconceivable aims, perverse activities. I knew their names, which so exactly fitted them as characters: the Jenny Hunderlegs, the gavelock, the forkytail, the slater – the underworld of my little underworld, obsessing me, but for ever beyond my reach. Some were not so horrible, such as the spider, impersonal compared with the others, whose progress was a terrifying dart or a grave, judge-like, swaying walk. Unlike the others, he was at home in the sun, and so did not need to scuttle; I thought of him as bearded and magistral. I could never bear to touch any of these creatures, though I watched them so closely that I seemed to be taking part in their life, which was like little fragments of night darting about in the sun; they often came into my dreams later, wakening me in terror. How many hours I must have spent staring with fixed loathing at these creatures! Yet I did not want to know anything about them; I merely wanted them away. Their presence troubled me as the mind is troubled in adolescence by the realization of physical lust. The gavelocks and forkytails were my first intimation of evil, and associations of evil still cling round them for me, as, I fancy, for most people: popular imagery shows it. We cannot tell how much our minds are influenced for life by the fact that we see the world first at a range of two or three feet.

The insects, of course, were only a small part of that three-foot world; I think I must have passed through a phase of possession by them, comparatively short. The grass was a reliable pleasure; the flowers were less dependable, and after I picked a dandelion one day and found it writhing with little angry, many-legged insects, the faces of the flowers took on a faithless look, until my mother taught me which could be relied upon. The crevices in stone walls were filled with secrets; a slab of hard cement on the wall of the house had a special meaning. Mud after new rain was delicious, and I was charmed by everything that flew, from the humble bee to the Willie

Longlegs. At that stage the novelty of seeing a creature flying outweighed everything else.

My height from the ground determined my response to other things too. When my father and Sutherland brought in the horses from the fields I stood trembling among their legs, seeing only their great, bearded feet and the momentary flash of their crescent-shaped shoes flung up lazily as they passed. When my father stopped with the bridle in his hands to speak to me I stood looking up at the stationary hulks and the tossing heads, which in the winter dusk were lost in the sky. I felt beaten down by an enormous weight and a real terror; yet I did not hate the horses as I hated the insects; my fear turned into something else, for it was infused by a longing to go up to them and touch them and simultaneously checked by the knowledge that their hoofs were dangerous: a combination of emotions which added up to worship in the Old Testament sense. Everything about them, the steam rising from their soft, leather nostrils, the sweat staining their hides, their ponderous, irresistible motion, the distant rolling of their eyes, which was like the revolution of rock-crystal suns, the waterfall sweep of their manes, the ruthless flick of their cropped tails, the plunge of their iron-shod hoofs striking fire from the flagstones, filled me with a stationary terror and delight for which I could get no relief. One day two of our horses began to fight in the field below the house, rearing at each other like steeds on a shield and flinging out with their hind-legs, until Sutherland rushed out to separate them. A son of our neighbour at the Haa had a crescent mark on his forehead where a horse had kicked him; I stared at it in entrancement, as if it were a sign in the sky. And in a copy of *Gulliver's Travels* which my eldest brother had won as a school prize there was a picture of a great horse sitting on a throne judging a crowd of naked men with hairy, hangdog faces. The horse was sitting on its hindquarters, which had a somewhat mean and inadequate appearance; its front hoofs were upraised and its neck arched as if to strike; and though the picture was strange and frightening, I took it to be the record of some actual occurrence. All this added to my terror of horses, so that I loved and dreaded them as an explorer loves and dreads a strange country which he has not yet entered.

I had no fear of the cows, and wandered confidently among their legs. There seemed to be no danger *in* cows, as there was in horses, nothing to fear except their size and weight; I could not imagine a cow sitting in judgement on a throne. I did not fear the big black, curly-browed bull either as I feared the horses; I merely felt wary of him, knowing that he was dangerous in a comprehensible way, and that my father and Sutherland approached him with caution. One evening early in summer he followed an old woman from a neigh-bouring farm as she was walking to the Bu. I was standing with my two sisters at the end of the house, and as the old woman drew near, walking quite slowly, we saw the black bull rollicking behind her, flinging up his heels raffishly and shaking his head, nonplussed because she never altered her pace. She was deaf and did not hear him. He pulled up before he reached her, and my sister called the dog Prince and drove him off. To the three of us there was something extravagantly funny in the sight of the old woman walking quietly along and the bull prancing behind her; but my father was alarmed, and on Sutherland's advice decided that the bull would have to wear a ring in his nose. The bull was dragged by a strong rope into the shed where the farm implements were kept. All the young men of Wyre gathered; it was a long, clear summer evening, and every sound could be heard for miles. The bull was fastened by stout ropes with his body inside the shed and his head and neck sticking through a window. The young men hung on to a cord fastened behind his ears to hold his head down, and Sutherland came round the corner of the byre with a red-hot iron in his hand. At that point my father drove me into the house, and Sutherland playfully threatened to scorch the roof of my mouth with the iron, saying that it would make me sing better; that frightened me, and I ran. I listened inside the kitchen door to the shouting of the men and the bellowing of the bull, which seemed to fill the island. When it stopped I went out again. The bull's head was still sticking through the window; there was a look of deep surprise on his face, and drops that looked like tears were rolling from his eyes; he kept tossing his head as if to shake off the neat, shining ring sticking in his nose. The ring, like everything new, delighted me. The men stood discussing the job in thoughtful voices. A chain was fixed to the ring, and after that the bull had to drag it after him wherever he went.

That summer my father took me one evening to the Haa with him. The farmer of the Haa had bought a cow and had just let it into the field where his other cows were grazing. He and his sons were standing at the gate of the field to watch how the herd would welcome the new cow. For a while the cows paid no attention; then they all began to look in the same direction and drew together as if for protection or consultation, staring at the strange cow, which had retreated into a corner of the field. Suddenly they charged in a pack, yet as if they were frightened, not angry. The farmer and his sons rushed into the field, calling on their dog, and managed to head off the herd. The new cow, trembling, was led back to the byre. My father and the farmer philosophically discussed the incident as two anthropologists might discuss the customs of strange tribes. It seemed that this treatment of new members of the herd was quite common. It frightened me, yet it did not shake my belief in the harmlessness of our own cows, but merely made me despise them a little for being subject to foolish impulses, for as they charged across the field they looked more foolish than dangerous.

The distance of my eyes from the ground influenced my image of my father and mother too. I have a vivid impression of my father's cream-coloured moleskin breeches, which resisted elastically when I flung myself against them, and of my mother's skirt, which yielded, softly enveloping me. But I cannot bring back my mental impression of them, for it is overlaid by later memories in which I saw them as a man and a woman, like, or almost like, other men and women. I am certain that I did not see them like this at first; I never thought that they were like other men and women; to me they were fixed allegorical figures in a timeless landscape. Their allegorical changelessness made them more, not less, solid, as if they were condensed into something more real than humanity; as if the image 'mother' meant more than 'woman', and the image 'father' more than 'man'. It was the same with my brothers and sisters, my cousin Sutherland, and my aunt Maggie. We begin life not by knowing men and women, but a father and a mother, brothers and sisters. Men and women, and mankind in general, are secondary images, for we know them first as strangers; but our father and mother were never strangers to us, nor our brothers and sisters if we were the last born, as I was. When I was a child I must have felt that they had always been there, and I with them, since I could not account for myself; and now I can see them only as a stationary pattern, changing, yet always the same, not as a number of separate people all following the laws of their different natures. Where all was stationary my mother came first; she certainly had always been with me in a region which could never be known again. My father came next, more recognizably in my own time, yet rising out of changelessness like a rock out of the sea. My brothers and sisters were new creatures like myself, not in time (for time still sat on the wrist of each day with its wings folded), but in a vast, boundless calm. I could not have put all this into words then, but this is what I felt and what we all feel before we become conscious that time moves and that all things change. That world was a perfectly solid world, for the days did not undermine it but merely rounded it, or rather repeated it, as if there were only one day endlessly rising and setting. Our first childhood is the only time in our lives when we exist within immortality, and perhaps all our ideas of immortality are influenced by it. I do not mean that the belief in immortality is a mere rationalization of childish impressions; I have quite other reasons for holding it. But we think and feel and believe immortally in our first few years, simply because time does not exist for us. We pay no attention to time until he tugs us by the sleeve or claps his policeman's hand on our shoulder; it is in our nature to ignore him, but he will not be ignored.

I can see my father quite clearly still with my later sight, though he has been dead for fifty years. He was a little, slight man with the soft brown beard of one who had never used a razor. His head was inclined sideways like the heads of statues of medieval saints; this had a natural cause, a contracted neck muscle; yet it seemed merely the outward mark of his character, which was gentle and meditative. His face was narrowish, with a long, delicate nose and large, fastidious lips almost hidden by his beard. He was slightly deaf and very embarrassed by it, and this may have been the reason why he was so fond of talking to himself. He would hold long conversations in the fields when no one was near; dialogues or monologues, I do not know which; but one could tell by the posture of his body and an occasional pensive wave of the hand that he was occupied. He was a religious man, but not strict or ostentatiously pious; he attended church irregularly but reverently; he often omitted grace before meals for long stretches; then he would remember and begin again. Every Sunday night he gathered us together to read a chapter of the Bible and kneel down in prayer. These Sunday nights are among my happiest memories; there was a feeling of complete security and union among us as we sat reading about David or Elijah. My father's prayer, delivered in a sort of mild chant while we knelt on the floor, generally ran on the same lines; at one point there always came the words, for which I waited, 'an house not made with hands, eternal in the heavens.' As a young man he had been saved, but he was not confident of his salvation, and I once heard him saying to my mother that he wished he was as certain of going to heaven as Jock M., a strict elder. I think there was a touch of irony in his words.

My father never beat us, and whether he was unlike his neighbours in that I cannot say. A distant relation of ours, Willie D., a brave and pious man, beat his family mercilessly. My father regretted his harshness, and often told of a day when he had been walking home from church with Willie and another man, talking of their children, when the other man turned to Willie and said, 'Never lift your hand to a bairn in anger. Wait, and you may change your mind.' My father admired these words, and often repeated them. Yet Willie went on thrashing his family; why I do not know; perhaps in a sort of panic, terrified what might happen to them if the evil were not driven out of them.

He came to see us once in Wyre. As I had heard so much about him I kept staring at him in guilty curiosity. He was not a big man, as I had expected, being scarcely taller than my father, but deep-chested and powerful and deliberate in his movements. He had a gentle, handsome, sad face and a grave voice, and perhaps because I knew he was so harsh to his family and yet so gentle to me I worshipped him. He must have been very attractive to women, for children are often drawn to men by the same qualities as women are. A few years later he lost his life setting out to sea in a storm which no other man would face.

The worst punishment we knew was an occasional clip across the ears from my father's soft cap with the ear-flaps, which he always wore, outside and inside; and this never happened unless we were making an unbearable noise. Afterwards he would sit back looking ashamed. Like most gentle people he was long-suffering, but when his anger was roused it frightened us. It was roused against me only once, and that was after we left Wyre. I had been sliding on the mill-dam all one Sunday morning against his orders, and when I came back at dinner-time he threatened to thrash me with a rope-end if I did it again. I felt outraged; such a thing had never been heard of in our house before. But I knew that he was terrified that the ice might break and leave me to drown, for the mill-dam was deep. It may have been some such terrifying vision of the future that made Willie D. thrash his children, that and the common belief that evil can be beaten out of children – violently driven out with blows.

My mother had more practical sense than my father, but was just as gentle. I cannot remember ever hearing them exchanging a discourteous word or raising their voices to each other. Their form of address was 'boy' and 'lass,' as it is still in Orkney among men and women, no matter of what age. My mother had a greater regard for appearances than my father, and a deeper family sense; her children were always in the right to her. She was inclined to worry, and wanted us to 'get on'. She too had passed through a religious experience as a young woman, and had a deep respect for religion, but not the spontaneous piety of my father. Yet it was she who taught me the story of Jesus out of a child's book whose name I cannot remember. It must have been written in a vein of mawkish sentiment, for it gave me the impression that Jesus was always slightly ill, a pale invalid with the special gentleness of people who cannot live as others do. My mother often lamented, as she read from this book, that she no longer had another one called *The Peep o' Day*, and for a long time I carried about an imaginary picture of it; I could see the frontispiece showing a bearded Jesus in a wide cloak, bearing a lamb in His arms. But it lay in the past, in a place I could never reach.

My mother liked the hymns in the Moody and Sankey hymn-book, and on Sunday evenings we would sing these catchy, self-satisfied tunes together: 'Hold the fort, for I am coming', 'Dare to be a Daniel', 'Bringing in the sheaves'. I always disliked them, but this only made me sing them more loudly, as if that would rid me of my dislike. Revivalist Christianity was saturated at that time with ideas of self-help, and my mother's wish that we might 'get on' may have gone back to her conversion. A paper called the *Christian Herald*, which we got weekly, helped to encourage this. It contained every week a sermon by the Reverend Charles Haddon Spurgeon, and another by the Reverend Doctor Talmage, as well as a page of prophecies by the Reverend Doctor Baxter, in which the date of the Millennium was calculated by comparing texts from Scripture. These speculations on the Millennium sank deep into my mind, as I was to discover many years later. There were stories too, showing the virtues of thrift and the dangers of drinking. *From Log Cabin to White House*, a Smilesian biography of President Garfield, had somehow got into our small library. I read it, as I read everything else. We had, of course, *The Pilgrim's Progress*, a book which thoroughly terrified me; and as a young man my father had taken out Goldsmith's *Natural History* in monthly parts with coloured plates, as well as a book called *The Scots Worthies*, a collection of biographies of reformers and Covenanters, abundantly illustrated with woodcuts. It was badly written, biased, and untruthful, but it contained some exciting stories of heroism and endurance. At one time it was to be found in every farmhouse in Scotland.

My mother was fond of singing, and she did not confine herself to hymns, though she drew a strict distinction between sacred and 'carnal' songs. I sang all her songs, carnal and sacred, after her. I can recollect singing at a concert in the Wyre school when I was four and not yet in trousers; it was an old Scots ballad about James V and his habit of going among his people disguised as a gaberlunzie man, or beggar; but I can remember only the end of the tune now and the last four lines of the text:

> Then doon he loot his duddy cloots,
> An' doon he loot them fa',
> An' he glittered in go-o-old
> Far abune them a'.

This gave me a great sense of glory. Another old ballad of my mother began:

> Of all the ancient Scottish knights
> Of great and warlike name
> The bravest was Sir James the Rose,
> That knight o' mickle fame.

I have never come across it since. There were also popular songs of a hundred or half a hundred years before, ballads of the Peninsular and the Crimean Wars, one of them telling how 'we stormed the heights of Alma.' There were eighteenth-century broad sheet ballads too, sung in the monotonous rhythm which the ploughmen love, containing many verses such as

> He was a very gallant lad,
> But I'm sorry for to say
> That for some bad crime or other
> He was sent to Botany Bay.

My brother Johnnie, who had an irreverent mind, brought back one day a hymn which he had heard the Salvation Army singing in Kirkwall:

> My old companions, fare ye we-ell;
> I will not go-o with you to He-e-ell;
> I mean for ever with Christ to dwe-ell.
> Will you go-o, will you go?

He never sang it when my father or mother was there, but the rest of us were delighted by it. My mother had also a lovely old Cockney song; how it reached her I do not know:

> But, oh, she was as beautiful as a butterfly
> And as proud as a queen,
> Was pretty little Polly Perkins
> Of Paddington Green.

There was a great difference between the earlier and the later songs. The ballads about James V and Sir James the Rose had probably been handed down orally for hundreds of years; they were consequently sure of themselves and were sung with your full voice, as if you had always been entitled to sing them; but the later ones were chanted in a sort of literary way, in honour of the print in which they had originally come, every syllable of the English text carefully pronounced, as if it were an exercise. These old songs, rooted for so long in the life of the people, are now almost dead.

We had two fiddles in the house and a melodeon. My two eldest brothers played the fiddle, and we were all expert on the melodeon. John Ritch, our neighbour at the Haa, was a great fiddler in the traditional country style, and he had a trick of making the bow *dirl* on the strings which delighted us, especially in slow, ceremonious airs such as *The Hen's March to the Midden*. Then one year we were all caught with a passion for draughts, and played one another endlessly through the long winter evenings, always wary when we met Sutherland, for he had a trick of unobtrusively replacing his men on the board in impregnable positions after they had been captured. If we pointed this out to him he would either deny it loudly or else show amazement at seeing them there. When I think of our winters at the Bu they turn into one long winter evening round the stove – it was a black iron stove with scrollwork on the sides, standing well out into the kitchen – playing draughts, or listening to the fiddle or the melodeon, or sitting still while my father told of his witches and fairicks. The winter gathered us into one room as it gathered the cattle into the stable and the byre; the sky came closer; the lamps were lit at three or four in the afternoon, and then the great evening lay before us like a world: an evening filled with talk, stories, games, music, and lamplight.

The passing from this solid winter world into spring was wild, and it took place on the day when the cattle were unchained from their stalls in the six months' darkness of the byre, and my father or Sutherland flung open the byre door and leaped aside. The cattle shot through the opening, blind after half a year's night, maddened by the spring air and the sunshine, and did not stop until they were brought up by the stone dyke at the other end of the field. If anyone had come in their way they would have trampled over him without seeing him. Our dog Prince, who kept a strict watch over them during the summer, shrank before the sight. That was how spring began.

There were other things connected with it, such as the lambing; I think our lambs must have been born late in the season. I have a picture of my mother taking me by the hand one green spring day and leading me to the yard at the back of the house to see two new-born lambs. Some bloody, wet, rag-like stuff was lying on the grass, and a little distance away the two lambs were sprawling with their spindly legs doubled up. Everything looked soft and new – the sky, the sea, the grass, the two lambs, which seemed to have been cast up without warning on the turf; their eyes still had a bruised look, and their hoofs were freshly lacquered. They paid no attention to me when I went up to pat them, but kept turning their heads with sudden gentle movements which belonged to some other place.

Another stage in the spring was the sowing. About that time of the year the world opened, the sky grew higher, the sea deeper, as the summer colours, blue and green and purple, woke in it. The black fields glistened, and a row of meal-coloured sacks, bursting full like the haunches of plough-horses, ran down each one; two neat little lugs, like pricked ears, stuck up from each sack. They were opened; my father filled from the first of them a canvas tray strapped round his middle, and strode along the field casting the dusty grain on either side with regular sweeps, his hands opening and shutting. When the grain was finished he stopped at another sack and went on again. I would sit watching him, my eyes caught now and then by some ship passing so slowly against the black hills that it seemed to be stationary, though when my attention returned to it again I saw with wonder that it had moved. The sun shone, the black field glittered, my father strode on, his arms slowly swinging, the fan-shaped cast of grain gleamed as it fell and fell again; the row of meal-coloured sacks stood like squat monuments on the field. My father took a special delight in the sowing, and we all felt the first day was a special day. But spring was only a few vivid happenings, not a state, and before I knew it the motionless blue summer was there, in which nothing happened.

There are zones of childhood through which we pass, and we live in several of them before we reach our school age, at which a part of our childhood stops for good. I can distinguish several different kinds of memory during my first seven years. There is first my memory of lying watching the beam of light, which I associate with no period and when I still seemed to be in the cradle. After that come my memories of the baptism and the singing at the concert; these belong to my petticoat stage, when I was conscious of myself as a small child moving safely among enormous presences. Next – as if my mother's fitting me out with trousers had really changed me – I remember myself as a boy, aware that I was different from little girls; no longer in the world where there is no marriage or giving in marriage.

This stage seems to have coincided with an onset of pugnacity, for my first memory of it is a fight with another boy over a knife. The memory is dim, and the figures in it huge and shadowy, making me think of the figures in the Scottish ballads, the Douglases and Percys. It must have been in autumn, for a sad light hangs over it. The other boy, whose name was Freddie, was standing with me at a place where two narrow roads crossed, and a little distance away two older girls with cloths over their heads were watching. Dusk was falling; the wet clouds hung just over our heads, shutting us in and making a small circular stage for the combat. I remember my anger rising and lifting my hand to strike. I knocked Freddie down and snatched the knife from him. He did not get up again, and that frightened me. I went over and shook him by the shoulder, and saw that he was crying as he lay with his face in the damp grass. A doctor had been to the house a little while before to attend to my mother, and I decided to be a doctor, went over to Freddie again, pretended to feel his pulse, and declared that he had recovered. How it ended and what became of the knife I do not remember.

This memory belongs to a different world from my other memories, perhaps because my pugnacious phase lasted only a short time, for after an attack of influenza I became timid and frightened. Other things as well may have helped to bring this about: I can give no clear explanation of it. In an island everything is near, for compressed within it are all the things which are spread out over a nation or a continent, and there is no way of getting away from them. A neighbouring farmer who had often brought me sweets in his snuff-lined pockets had died in great pain a little time before, and I had heard all about his death: I can still feel the terror of it. I have often fancied, too, that in a child's mind there is at moments a divination of a hidden tragedy taking place around him, that tragedy being the life which he will not live for some years still, though it is there, invisible to him, already. And a child has also a picture of human existence peculiar to himself, which he probably never remembers after he has lost it: the original vision of the world. I think of this picture or vision as that of a state in which the earth, the houses on the earth, and the life of every human being are related to the sky overarching them; as if the sky fitted the earth and the earth the sky. Certain dreams convince me that a child has this vision, in which there is a completer harmony of all things with each other than he will ever know again. There comes a moment (the moment at which childhood passes into boyhood or girlhood) when this image is broken and contradiction enters life. It is a phase of emotional and mental strain, and it brings with it a sense of guilt. All these things, the death of a man I knew, the sense of an unseen tragedy being played out around me, the destruction of my first image of the world, the attack of influenza, may have together brought about the change.

In any case I became timid and frightened. Of the influenza all I remember is the sweetish taste of the medicine; it seemed to taste of the metal teaspoon which I took it out of, and like the spoon was a light golden colour.

My phase of acute childish guilt – how long it lasted I do not know; it may have been months or merely weeks – was associated with a sack of sheep-dip which my father had brought from Kirkwall. As the dip was poisonous the sack was left in the middle of a field some distance from the house; my father gave us strict orders not to go near it and on no account to touch it. I took care to keep away from it; yet after the sheep had been dipped and the sack destroyed I could not feel certain that I had not touched it, and as I took my father's words literally, and thought that even to touch the sack might bring death, I went about in terror. For my hands might have touched the sack. How could I know, now that the sack was gone and I had no control over the boy who might have touched it or might not have touched it, being quite unable to stay his hand in that other time and that other place? My fear was beyond any argument, so I washed my hands many times a day, until they had a wasted, transparent look, and pored upon them afterwards in a sort of agony, as if I were trying to read something from them. My fear went about with me, never leaving me: I would turn corners to get away from it, or shut myself in a little closet with one window, where there seemed to be no room except for myself; but the closet was big enough to hold my fear too. Sometimes I would run for a long way to escape from it, until I could run no farther, and if I fell and cut my knee I felt that the blood trickling down must take me back to the ordinary world where other children too cut their knees and bled. My mother often looked anxiously at me, as if she thought I had gone away from her and she could not follow me; I often surprised that look in her face. And I had actually gone away into a world where every object was touched with fear, yet a world of the same size as the ordinary world and corresponding to it in every detail: a sort of parallel world divided by an endless, unbreakable sheet of glass from the actual world. For though my world was exactly the same in appearance as that world, I knew that I could not break through my fear to it, that I was invisibly cut off, and this terrified and bewildered me. The sense that I was in a blind place was always with me; yet that place was only a clear cloud or bubble surrounding me, from which I could escape at any moment by doing something; but what that was I did not know. My sister, playing in the sun a few feet away, was in that other world; my brothers cut and gathered the hay in it, the ships passed, the days followed one another in it. I could not reach it by getting close to it, though I often tried; for when my mother took me in her arms and laid my head on her shoulder she, so close to me, was in that world, and yet I was outside. How long this lasted I cannot tell, but at last the actual world appeared again in twisted gleams, as through running glass, and the fear and the frenzied longing to cleanse myself went away.

I cannot account for this passion of fear and guilt; perhaps at the root of it was the obsession which all young children have with sex, their brooding curiosity, natural in itself, but coloured with guilt by the thoughts of their elders. Children live in two worlds: in their own and that of grown-up people. What they do in their own world seems natural to them; but in the grown-up world it may be an incomprehensible yet deadly sin. A child has to believe things before he can prove them, often before he can understand them; it is his way of learning about the world, and the only way. Accordingly he can believe that he is sinning without feeling that he is sinning; but the sin, accepted at first on trust and made plausible by make-believe, may later take on an overwhelming imaginative reality, and guilt may fall upon him from an empty sky. The worst thing about my fears was that I could not tell my father and mother about them, since I did not understand them; and the knowledge that there were things in which their help, no matter how willing, could be of no use to me bewildered me most of all. When that film dissolved, the world my eyes saw was a different world from my first childish one, which never returned again. This fit of guilt and terror came when I was seven, and in summer, for it is associated with bright, glassy, windless weather. I know I was seven, for we had just moved from the Bu to the neighbouring farm of Helzigartha, or Helye, where we stayed only for a year.

A farm is such a carnival of birth and death, there is no wonder that it should frighten a child. With my first sight of the two lambs that foreign, dirty-red, rag-like stuff is associated like a stain, and I still cannot see them without seeing it. Perhaps if it had not been for the attack of influenza I might have thought less of it, might have tucked it into that non-committal pocket of the mind where, when our bodies are sound and our senses working normally, we put away what startles or disgusts us. I must have been convalescent at the time, with the pitiless hypersensitiveness of convalescence. Yet these first fears, coming from things so bound up with life, were probably good, and a child could not grow up in a better place than a farm; for at the heart of human civilization is the byre, the barn, and the midden. When my father led out the bull to serve a cow brought by one of our neighbours it was a ritual act of the tradition in which we have lived for thousands of years, possessing the obviousness of a long dream from which there is no awaking. When a neighbour came to stick the pig it was a ceremony as objective as the rising and setting of the sun; and though the thought never entered his mind that without that act civilization, with its fabric of customs and ideas and faiths, could not exist – the church, the school, the council chamber, the drawing-room, the library, the city – he did it as a thing that had always been done, and done in a certain way. There was a necessity in the copulation and the killing which took away the sin, or at least, by the ritual act, transformed it into a sad, sanctioned duty.

My mother always kept us in the house when cows were brought to the bull; we would listen to the shouts of the men in the yard with very little idea of what was happening, for the shouts were like the shouts of warriors or of men playing some heroic game. My mother tried to keep me in too when the pig was killed – I must have been about seven the first time – but I slipped out when her back was turned, ran over to the byre, and from a window there stared into the yard. The farmer who acted as pig-killer for the island was a strong, sandy-haired man with a great round lump on the side of his neck, from which a sheaf of lighter bristles, somewhat like a pig's, stuck out. He always brought his gully with him, a large, broad-bladed knife with a sharp point and a wooden handle. When I reached the window the pig had a great gash in its throat, and blood was frothing from it into a basin which Sutherland was holding in his hands as he knelt on one knee on the ground. My father and the farmer were clinging to the pig to keep it still; but suddenly it broke loose, knocking Sutherland down; the basin toppled over; the blood poured over the ground, and Sutherland rose cursing, wiping his red hands on his trousers. It was a bright, windy day, and little flurries and ripples ran over the pool of blood. The pig seemed to be changed. It flew on, quite strange to me, as if seeking something, with an evil, purposive look, as if it were a partner in the crime, an associate of the pig-killer. As it ran it kept up a saw-like screaming which seemed to come from the slit in its throat. It stopped now and then to consider what it should do next; for it was not acting at random, but with a purpose which I could not fathom, and which therefore frightened me. Once it stopped to sniff at a docken in a corner of the yard, and then it looked like itself again and I was not afraid of it. But at once it made another stumbling charge, and what glared out of its eyes was mortal cruelty, the cruelty of the act itself, the killing. Then it began to make little top-heavy lurches; every moment it seemed about to fall forward on its snout. I ran into the house and hid my face, crying, in my mother's skirt. She scolded me and comforted me.

Later, in memory, it seemed to me that I had pitied the pig; but I know that I did not; my terror was too great, and what I felt for it was hatred, for the pig seemed formidable and evil, except for the moment when it stopped to sniff at the docken. I did not go out again, and when, much later, the pig-killer came into the kitchen, his arms red with blood up to the elbows, to wash in a basin of hot water, I crawled under the table. He tried to coax me out, but I would not come. Later I went out to the barn, where the pig, neatly slit open, was hanging from the rafters by two cords passed through the sinews of its hind-legs. A warm, sweet smell filled the place, making me feel giddy; in a tub the entrails were floating in water; the pig swayed; the rafters creaked softly, as they did when we swung from them; the inside of the pig was pink and clean, with little frills and scallops of fat like convoluted shells running down either side. There was no one there but myself and the dead pig. I stared at it as at some infamous mystery and went away.

When I returned to the house Sutherland was sitting on a stool blowing up the bladder through a straw. It hung limp and purse-like for a moment; then it gradually filled; thin red veins stood out, stretching, on the stretched surface, which changed, growing thinner and thinner, like a gross bubble. He blew and blew, then tied a piece of string round the neck of the bladder and flung it to me. I dropped it, for it felt wet and slippery and had a strong smell. In a few days it grew stiff and dry, and I used it now and then as a football.

My memory of Sutherland killing a sheep in the barn is dim and ignominious, perhaps because Sutherland was an amateur and approached the business in a jaunty, conspiratorial vein. I have an impression of darkness and silence, as if the barn door had been closed to shut out the light and hide the deed; and I can see no one there but Sutherland and myself, which is so improbable that it must be due to a trick of memory. I can see the ewe lying on a bench on its side, meek and stupid, and Sutherland standing with a penknife in his hand, an infamously small penknife it seems to me now, though that must be another trick of memory. The whole scene is shameful, and gives me a feeling of cowardly stealth; I can remember nothing more about it.

Fortunately the barn was associated with happier memories, for about the same time Hughie o' Habreck, who was a skilled joiner as well as a farmer, came to build a yawl for my father. He was thickset and very strong, with a deep, rumbling voice and mutton-chop whiskers: a slow, consequential man who whenever he spoke seemed to be delivering a verdict, so that people were always asking his advice. He would stand over the growing boat and deliberate for a long time on what he should do next, at last saying in a judicial voice, as if he had just convinced himself, 'We'll do this now,' or 'We'll do that now.' He was never in a hurry; he sawed and planed and chiselled in a particular way of his own, absorbed in the thought of the boat, as if there were nothing but it and himself in the world, and his relation to it had a complete, objective intimacy. I cannot remember much about the actual building of the boat, except for the bending of the boards in steam, the slow growth of the sides as one smooth ply of wood was set on another, the sides bulging in a more swelling curve from bow to stern as the days passed in delicious slowness, the curly shavings, the scent of wood and resin, and a pot of bubbling tar into which you could thrust your hand without being burned if you dipped your hand in water first. The boat was eventually finished, and my brothers often went out in it in the evenings to fish, taking me with them.

I must have been seven when the great storm came. I can still remember distinctly the first day, which was dull and windless, the sky filled with clouds which hung without movement, like the full, suspended sails of a great fleet, yet seemed to expand and to be forced lower and lower as the darkness fell, until they were just over my head. I was coming back from school when, as I passed the little pond below the house, I became aware of the intense stillness: I can see myself for that moment; before and after there is a blank. When I went into the kitchen my mother said that she did not like the look of the weather, which surprised me, for I had loved the dull, sad stillness, the dense air which made each motionless blade of grass sweat one clear drop, the dreary immobility of the pond. A little while afterwards we heard an iron pail flying with a great clatter along the length of the house. My father and Sutherland ran out to see that all the doors and windows of the steading were fast shut. I wanted to go with them to see the storm, but my mother forbade me, saying that the wind would blow me away: I took it for a fictitious warning for I did not know then that wind could do such things. The storm itself made very little impression on me, for I was in the house, and looking out of the windows I could not see that there was anything to see except the dull sky with its low-flying clouds, and the flattened look of everything, and the desertion of the fields. On the second day Sutherland reported that a boat anchored in the sound had dragged its anchor for several miles. This seemed to impress him and my father a great deal, and I tried to be impressed too. But what really excited me was the knowledge that this was a storm, and not merely a wind; for I thought of a storm as something different from a wind. The storm must have lasted for several days; when the wind fell news came across from Rousay that a boat returning from the mainland with two men and two women had been lost on the first day. The sea was still high, but my father and Sutherland set out in our boat, along with the other boats of Wyre and Rousay, to look for the drowned party. In the evening Sutherland talked of what the sea did to the dead, swelling their bodies and sending them to the surface on the third day. Other cases of drowning came up; at that time, when most farmers had a share in a boat and went out in the fishing season, death at sea was common in Orkney. The bodies were eventually found.

It was about the time when my first world was crumbling and I was frightened and ill that I was sent to school. This was not until I was seven, on account of bad health. I had come very little in contact with other boys, but had struck up a great friendship with a little girl at a neighbouring farm who was a year younger than myself. What we did and what games we played I cannot remember now; but we were together every day throughout the summer, and often played for hours in the roofless chapel, where the weeds were as tall as ourselves. It was not one of those precocious imitative love affairs which seem to waken in children of that age if their parents so much as suggest it. We were very friendly; we hardly ever quarrelled, for there was no rivalry between us. Our friendship was more intimate than a friendship between two boys of the same age would have been; it was more quiet and settled too; very like the friendship of an old married couple. Sometimes it was interrupted by bouts of showing off; but these never lasted long, for we found they spoiled everything. What we could have done during all these long summer days, how we could have filled in the time with enjoyment, effortlessly, as in a dream, I cannot imagine. My brothers and sisters were all at the school, so that we were left quite to ourselves day after day.

Out of this friendship I was flung into the school, a small school with only fifteen or sixteen pupils, but all of them strange. The teacher – I had often sat on her knee when she came to see us at the Bu – was kind to me, but I soon realized that she was different in the classroom, and it took me a long time to understand why. I was a backward child, good at nothing but singing; and the examiner who visited the school at the end of my first summer term was so disappointed with my answers that he said in a more formidable voice than I had ever heard in my life before, 'This must be a particularly stupid boy.' He was a tall, big-faced man in a brown tweed suit smelling of peat, and his large hands were terribly scrubbed and clean.

I disliked school from the start. The classroom which had to serve us all, with its smell of ink, chalk, slate pencils, corduroy, and varnish, made me feel as if my head were stuffed with hot cotton-wool, and I realized quite clearly that I was caught and there was no escape. A map of the world covered one of the walls, a small, drab world, smaller even than the classroom; the light brown benches with the inkpots let into them seemed too hard and new; the windows showed nothing but the high clouds floating past. Time moved by minute degrees there; I would sit for a long time invisibly pushing the hands of the clock on with my will, and waken to realize that they had scarcely moved. I was afraid of the other boys at first, who seemed to have grown up in a different world from mine. Gradually I made friends with the younger ones on an uneasy footing which might crumble at any moment without my knowing why. Some of my dread and dislike of school was certainly due to bad health.

I had to leave for Edinburgh by the morning train a few years ago – I was living at St Andrews at the time – and as I walked to the station I passed the children going to school. It was a dismal morning draped with discoloured rags of clouds like a great washing; a few drops of rain splashed down at meaningless intervals; sodden leaves were plastered to the pavements and low walls. I watched the children, their satchels on their backs, walking through the school gate and trudging towards a door in the high wall; there was little sound anywhere, for it was an unfrequented street; everything had an air of secrecy. I can give no idea of the dreariness of the scene; the earth bleared and wet; the dejected children. I seemed to see an enormous school, higher even than this one, and millions of children all over the world creeping towards it and disappearing into it. The picture rose of itself, and it brought back a still Sunday evening in Wyre, when my mother and I had gone for a walk. The walk took us past the school, which, being shut, had a clean, forsaken look. My heart beat faster as we drew near, and I looked with dread at the ragged grass of the playground, not pounded now by the boots of the other boys, but lying peaceful and lost. I lingered to glance at the classroom windows, and my head grew hot and tight, as if I had been shut in a clothes cupboard. That was the feeling which my first year at school gave me, a feeling of being shut in some narrow, clean, wooden place: it must be known to every one who has attended a school, and the volume of misery it has caused will not bear thinking of. One day it made me so sick that Miss Angus took me outside and told me to sit down in a grassy field. It was a warm summer day. She came out later and told me to go home.

The day I remember best was the day when Freddie Sinclair chased me home: it was after we had gone to Helye, and his road lay in the same direction as mine. He was the boy I had fought over the knife, and this day he wanted to fight me again, but I was afraid. The road from the school to Helye lay on the crown of the island, and as I ran on, hollow with fear, there seemed to be nothing on either side of me but the sky. What I was so afraid of I did not know; it was not Freddie, but something else; yet I could no more have turned and faced him than I could have stopped the sun revolving. As I ran I was conscious only of a few huge things, monstrously simplified and enlarged: Wyre, which I felt under my feet, the other islands lying round, the sun in the sky, and the sky itself, which was quite empty. For almost thirty years afterwards I was so ashamed of that moment of panic that I did not dare to speak of it to anyone, and drove it out of my mind. I was seven at the time, and in the middle of my guilty fears. On that summer afternoon they took the shape of Freddie Sinclair, and turned him into a terrifying figure of vengeance. I felt that all the people of Wyre, as they worked in their fields, had stopped and were watching me, and this tempered my fear with some human shame. I hoped that none of my family had noticed me, but when they came in from the fields at tea-time Sutherland said, 'Weel, boy, I see thu can run!' I had got over my panic by then, and pretended that Freddie and I had been merely having a race. Sutherland laughed. 'Ay, a fine race, man, a fine race!' He called me 'man' when he wanted to be sarcastic.

I got rid of that terror almost thirty years later in a poem describing Achilles chasing Hector round Troy, in which I pictured Hector returning after his death to run the deadly race over again. In the poem I imagined Hector as noticing with intense, dreamlike precision certain little things, not the huge simplified things which my conscious memory tells me I noticed in my own flight. The story is put in Hector's mouth:

> The grasses puff a little dust
> Where my footsteps fall,
> I cast a shadow as I pass
> The little wayside wall.

> The strip of grass on either hand
> Sparkles in the light,
> I only see that little space
> To the left and to the right,

> And in that space our shadows run,
> His shadow there and mine,
> The little knolls, the tossing weeds,
> The grasses frail and fine.

That is how the image came to me, quite spontaneously: I wrote the poem down, almost complete, at one sitting. But I have wondered since whether that intense concentration on little things, seen for a moment as the fugitive fled past them, may not be a deeper memory of that day preserved in a part of my mind which I cannot tap for ordinary purposes. In any case the poem cleared my conscience. I saw that my shame was a fantastically elongated shadow of a childish moment, imperfectly remembered; an untapped part of my mind supplied what my conscious recollection left out, and I could at last see the incident whole by seeing it as happening, on a great and tragic scale, to some one else. After I had written the poem the flight itself was changed, and with that my feelings towards it. A psychologist would say that this was because I had suppressed my knowledge of my cowardice, and that it could trouble me only so long as I suppressed it. That may be so, but what it was that made me stop suppressing it is another question. I think there must be a mind within our minds which cannot rest until it has worked out, even against our conscious will, the unresolved questions of our past; it brings up these questions when our will is least watchful, in sleep or in moments of intense contemplation. My feeling about the Achilles and Hector poem is not of a suppression suddenly removed, but rather of something which had worked itself out. Such events happen again and again in everyone's life; they may happen in dreams; they always happen unexpectedly, surprising us if we are conscious of them at the time. It is an experience as definite as conviction of sin; it is like a warning from a part of us which we have ignored, and at the same time like an answer to a question which we had not asked, or an unsolicited act of help where no help was known to be. These solutions of the past projected into the present, deliberately announced as if they were a sibylline declaration that life has a meaning, impress me more deeply than any other kind of experience with the conviction that life does have a meaning quite apart from the thousand meanings which the conscious mind attributes to it: an unexpected and yet incontestable meaning which runs in the teeth of ordinary experience, perfectly coherent, yet depending on a different system of connected relations from that by which we consciously live.

The winter before we left the Bu a curious thing happened. One of the farmers in Wyre, an old friend of my father's, had left, and a new tenant had come in his place. The new farmer was a big, fat, sandy-haired man with a face the colour of porridge and eyes with almost white lashes. He was coarse and overbearing, and the other farmers, being quiet, peaceable men, did not like him. He had a jeering, over-familiar way with him, and was fond of strolling across to his neighbours' fields and criticizing them while they worked, all under a cloak of jocularity. One winter evening a few months after he had come to the island the new farmer burst in upon us in great agitation. He had been coming from the shop, which was at the other end of Wyre. As he returned along the shore he decided to have a look at his boat and see that it was safe; it was a wild night and very dark. When he reached his boat he heard voices at the other side of it and stopped to listen. The voices belonged to two young lads, and the other one was trying to persuade the younger to take out the plug, so that when the farmer went out the boat would fill and drown him. The farmer jumped up with a shout and made for them, and the two boys ran off. He chased them half across the island, stumbling over dykes and falling into burns. When he reached the Bu he was in a dreadful state. My father was deeply shocked, for the boys were sons of close neighbours of ours. The farmer kept saying, 'I'll have the law o' him! I'll have the law o' him!' This raised him in my eyes, for to have the law of anyone was something we only read about in *The Orcadian* or *The People's Journal*. He praised the younger lad as an honest boy who would do nobody any harm, but when he came to the older one he kept saying, 'He's wicked! He's wicked!' in an incredulous voice, as if wickedness were a thing he did not expect to find in an island like Wyre. My father tried to pacify him and make him believe that the older boy had not meant it. But after the farmer left he said, 'That Willie A. is a bad, sly boy.' 'sly' was the worst word he could find for anyone. The scandal blew over somehow, and the farmer was treated more kindly by his neighbours afterwards.

During our last year at the Bu there was a wedding at one of the farms, and we were all invited to it. We went in the afternoon and returned early next morning. I remember the dancing in the lighted barn, and a crowd of young women who were unaccountably kind to me, pressing cakes upon me and filling my pockets with sweets until they stuck out at both sides. My strangest memory of the wedding is a vivid, dream-like glimpse of a young farm-servant, whom we called

Goliath of Gath, as he gazed at one of the girls. He was strong, proud of his strength, stupid, and always at a loss for a word. He had an ox-like head set on a strong neck. Large drops of sweat were rolling down his face, and his eyes seemed to be melting in a soft, invisible flame. I had never seen a look like that in a man's face before, and if I had known anything about adult passions I would have seen him as a shaven ox slowly basting in the fires of love. As it is, he is like a part of a mythological picture to me now, and a line which was left in my mind by a dream one morning some years ago probably came from that glimpse of his face more than forty years before. The line was:

Jove with the ponderous glory of the bull,

which is quite unlike any poetry that I write. I have always thought of Jove's brow as broad and a little stupid and yet glorious like that of a bull. I do not like the line; it is an echo, perhaps even a line unconsciously cribbed from some Elizabethan poet, though I do not know its source.

The dream itself was a curious one. I was in a town in Spain or Portugal (I have never been to Spain or Portugal). I was wandering about the streets in bright sunshine in a stiff, creased tweed suit, feeling annoyed that I was wearing a waistcoat; yet the heat was not so great as I had expected, though it made my face feel stiff and salt and sore. I had a soft felt hat pulled down over my brow. I could see myself objectively, without illusion, so that the figure did not seem to be really like me; more like an old friend.

As I walked along I was struck by a bas-relief on the gable of an old house. It represented an enormous muscular figure which I took to be Hercules; the body and limbs swelled out heavily yet resiliently from the wall like a great cluster of grapes, though it had the look too of an opulent heraldic inn-sign; there was a great deal of dark blue and purple surrounding the main figure, suggesting the wine-cup and the vine-press. It was like an ancient and rich relic which had survived the long, watery wash of Time from an age when animal and man and god lived densely together in the same world: the timeless, crowded age of organic heraldry. Somewhere in this picture, transfigured, was that young farm-servant in Wyre whose face, caught in a moment of animal glory, had been such a revelation. Yet I had not known at the time what the revelation was; I had merely seen the glow, the transformation, without understanding, in a sort of wonder. 'The ponderous glory of the bull' suggested Spain; the rich colours, which might have been either wine or blood, were colours of sacrifice and rejoicing; the Hercules himself was probably an idealization of the farm-servant, whom now, after forty years, I was offering up to some unknown ancestral god in my mind.

I have always been fascinated by a part of us about which we know far less than our remote ancestors did: the part which divined those immediate though concealed relations that made them endow their heroes with the qualities of the animals whose virtues they incarnated, calling a man a bull for strength, a lion for courage, or a fox for cunning. That age is fabulous to us, populated by heraldic men and legendary beasts. We see a reflection of it in the Indian reliefs where saints and crowned emperors wander among tigers, elephants, and monkeys, and in the winged bulls of the Assyrians with their human heads: angel, beast, and man in one. The age which felt this connexion between men and animals was so much longer than the brief historical period known to us that we cannot conceive it; but our unconscious life goes back into it. In that age everything was legendary, and the creatures went about like characters in a parable of beasts. Some of them were sacred and some monstrous, some quaint and ugly as house gods; they were worshipped and sacrificed; they were hunted; and the hunt, like the worship and the sacrifice, was a ritual act. They were protagonists in the first sylvan war, half human and half pelted and feathered, from which rose the hearth, the community, and the arts. Man felt guilty towards them, for he took their lives day after day, in obedience to a custom so long established that no one could say when it began. Though he killed them, they were sacred to him, because without destroying them he could not live; and so when they lay in heaps, in hecatombs, they were a vast sacrifice offered by the animal kingdom, and they gave their lives in hundreds of thousands, guiltlessly, by a decree of destiny.

Man tamed some of them and yoked them to the plough and the mill; he fattened them so that he might eat their flesh; he drank their milk, used their fleeces and their hides to clothe him, their horns as ornaments or goblets, and lived with them under the same roof. This went on for ages beside which the age we know is hardly more than a day. As their life had to be taken and the guilt for it accepted, the way of taking it was important, and the ritual arose, in which were united the ideas of necessity and guilt, turning the killing into a mystery.

My passion for animals comes partly from being brought up so close to them, in a place where people lived as they had lived for two hundred years; partly from I do not know where. Two hundred years ago the majority of people lived close to the animals by whose labour or flesh they existed. The fact that we live on these animals remains; but the personal relation is gone, and with it the very ideas of necessity and guilt. The animals we eat are killed by thousands in slaughter-houses which we never see. A rationalist would smile at the thought that there is any guilt at all: there is only necessity, he would say, a necessity which is laid upon all carnivores, not on man only. But our dreams and ancestral memories speak a different language. As it is, the vegetarians are more honest than the rest of us, though their alternative is probably a false one, for they merely avoid the guilt instead of accepting it.

I do not know whether many people have dreams of animals; perhaps these dreams die out in families which have lived for two or three generations in a big city; I have no means of knowing. But it is certain that people who have been brought up in close contact with animals, including the vast majority of the generations from whom we spring, have dreamed and dream of animals, and my own experience shows that these dreams are often tinged with a guilt of which consciously we are unaware. As I feel that these dreams go back to my world as a child, the best place to speak of them is here. If I were recreating my life in an autobiographical novel I could bring out these correspondences freely and show how our first intuition of the world expands into vaster and vaster images, creating a myth which we act almost without knowing it, while our outward life goes on in its ordinary routine of eating, drinking, sleeping, working, and making money in order to beget sons and daughters who will do the same. I could follow these images freely if I were writing an autobiographical novel. As it is, I have to stick to the facts and try to fit them in where they will fit in.

It is clear that no autobiography can begin with a man's birth, that we extend far beyond any boundary line which we can set for ourselves in the past or the future, and that the life of every man is an endlessly repeated performance of the life of man. It is clear for the same reason that no autobiography can confine itself to conscious life, and that sleep, in which we pass a third of our existence, is a mode of experience, and our dreams a part of reality. In themselves our conscious lives may not be particularly interesting. But what we are not and can never be, our fable, seems to me inconceivably interesting. I should like to write that fable, but I cannot even live it; and all I could do if I related the outward course of my life would be to show how I have deviated from it; though even that is impossible, since I do not know the fable or anybody who knows it. One or two stages in it I can recognize: the age of innocence and the Fall and all the dramatic consequences which issue from the Fall. But these lie behind experience, not on its surface; they are not historical events; they are stages in the fable.

The problem that confronts an autobiographer even more urgently than other men is, How can he know himself? I am writing about myself in this book, yet I do not know what I am. I know my name, the date and place of my birth, the appearance of the places I have lived in, the people I have met, the things I have done. I know something of the society which dictates many of my actions, thoughts, and feelings. I know a little about history, and can explain to myself in a rough-and-ready fashion how that society came into being. But I know all this in an external and deceptive way, as if it were a dry legend which I had made up in collusion with mankind. This legend is founded on a sort of agreement such as children presuppose in their games of make-believe: an agreement by which years and days are given certain numbers to distinguish them, and peoples and countries and other things certain names; all this is necessary, of course, for the business of living. But it is a deception as well: if I knew all these figures and names I should still not know myself, far less all the other people in the world, or the small number whom I call friends. This external approach, no matter how perfect, will never teach me much either about them or about myself.

Take the appearance of a man, which is supposed to tell so much about him. He can never see that appearance: he can never see himself. If he looks at his face in a mirror, which faithfully reflects not only him, but the anxiety or hope with which he stares into it, he does not feel that this is himself. The face he sees has a certain convincing quality, it is true, like all faces; there is experience, thought, evasion, resolution, success, failure, suffering, and a certain comfort in it; there is in it everything that one can ask from a face. It imposes without effort – there can be no doubt of that – on every one else. He knows that it was made by him and time in a curious, often reluctant collaboration, and time is so much the stronger partner that at certain moments there seems to be nothing there but time. For though he incised every line himself – with no idea that these lines would remain – time fixed each of them by a principle of selection which had no regard whatever for him. If he looks honestly at the result it is time that convinces him, time that tells him, 'You must accept this, for I have preserved it.' Yet what time preserves is not what he would have liked to preserve. So that there are moments when he is so oppressed by this face which he carries about wherever he goes that he would like to take it down and put it up again differently; but only death can do that. There is no getting away from this result of time's collaboration. This face constructed to look like a face has an absolute plausibility. Yet if the man sees that face in a photograph it looks like the face of a stranger.

Or take a man's actions. We may know that he works in an office or in a coal-mine, that he has made a great deal of money by speculating on the Stock Exchange, that he once reached the South Pole, that he governed a province in India, that he won a race, that he threw up his post to nurse lepers or save the souls of heathens. These things tell us something about him; working in an office, winning money on the Stock Exchange, reaching the South Pole, and converting heathens leave their mark on a man, and *condition* him. A clerk is not like a coal-miner, or a stockbroker like an explorer. It is the same with countless other things. A man who lives in Kensington is different from a man who lives in Wapping. The differences are important, and they are caused by various distortions. It distorts a man to work in a coal-mine or an office; it distorts him in a different way to make a fortune on the Stock Exchange, though in a commercial society the distortion may be less apparent. It needs not distort a man so much to be an explorer or a missionary. The miner cannot live a civilized life, and society sins against him; the stockbroker will not live a civilized life, and sins against society. Or at any rate the sin is there, though it is difficult to establish where its roots lie. These things are of enormous importance, and we shall never settle them until the miner and the stockbroker live a civilized life.

But they are not of much help to us when we set out to discover what we are, and there is a necessity in us, however blind and ineffectual, to discover what we are. Religion once supplied that knowledge, but our life is no longer ruled by religion. Yet we can know what we are only if we accept some of the hypotheses of religion. Human beings are understandable only as immortal spirits; they become natural then, as natural as young horses; they are absolutely unnatural if we try to think of them as a mere part of the natural world. They are immortal spirits distorted and corrupted in countless ways by the world into which they are born; bearing countless shapes, beautiful, quaint, grotesque; living countless lives, trivial, sensational, dull; serving behind counters, going to greyhound races, playing billiards, preaching to savages in Africa, collecting stamps, stalking deer in the Highlands, adding up figures in an office for fifty years, ruining one another in business, inventing explosives which will destroy other men and women on a large scale, praying for the cessation of war, weeping over their sins, or trying to discover what sin really is: doing everything that is conceivable for human beings to do, and doing it in a different way at every stage of history. I do not have the power to prove that man is immortal and that the soul exists; but I know that there must be such a proof, and that compared with it every other demonstration is idle. It is true that human life without immortality would be inconceivable to me, though that is not the ground for my belief. It would be inconceivable because if man is an animal by direct descent I can see human life only as a nightmare populated by animals wearing top-hats and kid gloves, painting their lips and touching up their cheeks and talking in heated rooms, rubbing their muzzles together in the moment of lust, going through innumerable clever tricks, learning to make and listen to music, to gaze sentimentally at sunsets, to count, to acquire a sense of humour, to give their lives for some cause, or to pray.

This picture has always been in my mind since one summer evening in Glasgow in 1919. I did not believe in the immortality of the soul at that time; I was deep in the study of Nietzsche, and had cast off with a great sense of liberation all belief in any other life than the life we live here and now, as an imputation on the purity of immediate experience, which I had intellectually convinced myself was guiltless and beyond good and evil. I was returning in a tramcar from my work; the tramcar was full and very hot; the sun burned through the glass on backs of necks, shoulders, faces, trousers, skirts, hands, all stacked there impartially. Opposite me was sitting a man with a face like a pig's, and as I looked at him in the oppressive heat the words came into my mind, 'That is an animal.' I looked round me at the other people in the tram-car; I was conscious that something had fallen from them and from me; and with a sense of desolation I saw that they were all animals, some of them good, some evil, some charming, some sad, some happy, some sick, some well. The tram-car stopped and went on again, carrying its menagerie; my mind saw countless other tram-cars where animals sat or got on or off with mechanical dexterity, as if they had been trained in a circus; and I realized that in all Glasgow, in all Scotland, in all the world, there was nothing but millions of such creatures living an animal life and moving towards an animal death as towards a great slaughter-house. I stared at the faces, trying to make them human again and to dispel the hallucination, but I could not. This experience was so terrifying that I dismissed it, deliberately forgot it by that perverse power which the mind has of obliterating itself. I felt as if I had lived for a few moments in Swift's world, for Swift's vision of humanity was the animal vision. I could not have endured it for more than a few minutes. I did not associate it at the time with Nietzsche. But I realized that I could not bear mankind as a swarming race of thinking animals, and that if there was not somewhere, it did not matter where – in a suburb of Glasgow or of Hong Kong or of Honolulu – a single living soul, life was a curious, irrelevant desolation. I pushed away this realization for a time, but it returned again later, like the memory of my cowardice as a boy.

The animal world is a great impersonal order, without pathos in its suffering. Man is bound to it by necessity and guilt, and by the closer bond of life, for he breathes the same breath. But when man is swallowed up in nature nature is corrupted and man is corrupted. The sense of corruption in *King Lear* comes from the fact that Goneril, Regan and Cornwall are merely animals furnished with human faculties as with weapons which they can take up or lay down at will, faculties which they have stolen, not inherited. Words are their teeth and claws, and thought the technique of the deadly spring. They are so *unnatural* in belonging completely to nature that Gloucester can explain them only by 'these late eclipses in the sun and moon'. In *King Lear* nature is monstrous because man has been swallowed up in it:

A serving-man, proud in heart and mind; that curled my hair; wore gloves in my cap; served the lust of my mistress' heart and did the act of darkness with her; swore as many oaths as I spake words and broke them in the sweet face of heaven: one that slept in the contriving of lust and waked to do it: wine loved I deeply, dice dearly, and in woman out-paramoured the Turk: false of heart, light of ear, bloody of hand; hog in sloth, fox in stealth, wolf in greediness, dog in madness, lion in prey.

That is a picture of an animal with human faculties, made corrupt and legendary by the proudly curled hair. The conflict in Lear is a conflict between the sacred tradition of human society, which is old, and nature, which is always new, for it has no background. As I sat in that tram-car in Glasgow I was in an unhistorical world; I was outside time without being in eternity; in the small, sensual, momentary world of a beast.

But I believe that man has a soul and that it is immortal, not merely because on any other supposition human life would be inconceivable and monstrous; for I know that there are many people who believe that man is merely a thinking animal and yet do not consider him monstrous, and that there are a few people who, believing this, consider him monstrous, but do not find him inconceivable: who accept the nightmare and acknowledge nothing beyond it, as Swift did. But I think there are not many people who have the strength to do this; the great majority of those who see man as a thinking animal cannot do so without idealizing him, without seeing him ascending to some transcendent height in some future: they are sentimentalists with a passionate faith in self-help. My belief in immortality, so far as I can divine its origin, and that is not far, seems to be connected with the same impulse which urges me to know myself. I can never know myself; but the closer I come to knowledge of myself the more certain I must feel that I am immortal, and, conversely, the more certain I am of my immortality the more intimately I must come to know myself. For I shall attend and listen to a class of experiences which the disbeliever in immortality ignores or dismisses as irrelevant to temporal life. The experiences I mean are of little practical use and have no particular economic or political interest. They come when I am least aware of myself as a personality moulded by my will and time: in moments of contemplation when I am unconscious of my body, or indeed that I have a body with separate members; in moments of grief or prostration; in happy hours with friends; and, because self-forgetfulness is most complete then, in dreams and day-dreams and in that floating, half-discarnate state which pre-cedes and follows sleep. In these hours there seems to me to be knowledge of my real self and simultaneously knowledge of immor-tality. Sleep tells us things both about ourselves and the world which we could not discover otherwise. Our dreams are part of experience;

earlier ages acknowledged this. If I describe a great number of dreams in this book I do so intentionally, for I should like to save from the miscellaneous dross of experience a few glints of immortality.

I have had many dreams about animals, domestic, wild, and legendary, but I shall describe only one at this point, as it seems to me to throw into an imaginative shape two of the things I have been writing about: our relation to the animal world, a relation involving a predestined guilt, and our immortality. All guilt seeks expiation and the end of guilt, and our blood-guiltiness towards the animals tries to find release in visions of a day when man and the beasts will live in friendship and the lion will lie down with the lamb. My dream was connected with this vision. I dreamed that I was lying asleep, when a light in my room wakened me. A man was standing by my bedside. He was wearing a long robe, which fell about him in motionless folds, while he stood like a column. The light that filled the room came from his hair, which rose straight up from his head, burning, like a motionless brazier. He raised his hand, and without touching me, merely by making that sign, lifted me to my feet in one movement, so that I stood before him. He turned and went out through the door, and I followed him. We were in the gallery of a cloister; the moon was shining, and the shadows of the arches made black ribs on the flagstones. We went through a street, at the end of which there was a field, and while we walked on the moonlight changed to the white light of early morning. As we passed the last houses I saw a dark, shabby man with a dagger in his hand; he was wearing rags bound round his feet, so that he walked quite soundlessly; there was a stain as of blood on one of his sleeves; I took him to be a robber or a murderer and was afraid. But as he came nearer I saw that his eyes, which were fixed immovably on the figure beside me, were filled with a profound, violent adoration such as I had never seen in human eyes before. Then, behind him, I caught sight of a confused crowd of other men and women in curious or ragged clothes, and all had their eyes fixed with the same look on the man walking beside me. I saw their faces only for a moment. Presently we came to the field, which as we drew near changed into a great plain dotted with little conical hills a little higher than a man's head. All over the plain animals were standing or sitting on their haunches on these little hills; lions, tigers, bulls, deer, elephants, were there; serpents too wreathed their lengths on the knolls; and each was separate and alone, and each slowly lifted its head upward as if in prayer. This upward-lifting motion had a strange solemnity and deliberation; I watched head after head upraised as if proclaiming some truth just realized, and yet as if moved by an irresistible power beyond them. The elephant wreathed its trunk upward, and there was something pathetic and absurd in that indirect act of adoration. But the other animals raised their heads with the inevitability of the sun's rising, as if they knew, like the sun, that a new day was about to begin, and were giving the signal for its coming. Then I saw a little dog busily running about with his nose tied to the ground, as if he did not know that the animals had been redeemed. He was a friendly little dog, officiously going about his business, and it seemed to me that he too had a place in this day, and that his oblivious concern with the earth was also a sort of worship. How the dream ended I do not remember: I have now only a memory of the great animals with all their heads raised to heaven.

I had this dream a long time after I left Orkney; I was living in London and being psychoanalysed. I had so many dreams about this time that I could hardly keep count of them. In a great number of them I encountered dragons and mythological monsters, the explanation of the analyst being that I had for many years suppressed the animal in myself, so that it could come up now only in these wild and terrifying shapes. He was right up to a point in assuming this, for I had grown up a Puritan, and though I had liberated my mind, my senses were still bound. But he was right only up to a point, for the strange thing about these monsters was that they did not terrify me; instead I felt in a curious way at home with them. I can remember only one of them that frightened me: a great roaring sea-beast which I was trying to fight with an oar as I stood in a boat. I have had many dreams of fear, but except for this one hardly any of them have been connected with animals. It seems to me that most of the dreams I had about this time were ancestral dreams or Millennial dreams like the one I have just described. Our minds are possessed by three mysteries: where we came from, where we are going, and, since we are not alone, but members of a countless family, how we should live with one another. These questions are aspects of one question, and none of them can be separated from the others and dealt with alone. In my dream about the animals all three questions are involved; for the dream touches the relation between man and the animals and points to his origin, while in the image of the animal kingdom glorified and reconciled with mankind it points simultaneously to man's end, and with that to the way in which he should live in a society, for that question is inseparable from the question of his end.

There were Millennial airs in that dream, or, in the analyst's words, themes from the racial unconscious. But there was also in it something of my first few years; the hills were the little green hills of childhood; the figure who appeared by my bedside was a childish image of Christ; and the event itself, the Millennium, had often been discussed by my father and mother at the Bu after a reading of the Reverend Doctor Baxter, while I listened and almost without knowing it fashioned my own delightful pictures, long since forgotten. There was a great deal of Biblical discussion in our house, and the brazier of burning hair may be a far-off reminiscence of a long debate between me and my Aunt Maggie, who was a tough casuist, on the translation of Elijah to heaven. That summer D., the husband of a relative of my mother who lived in Edinburgh, had come to Orkney for his holidays, and stayed for a while at the Bu. He was a commercial traveller, a good violinist, and a man of some intelligence, with an inflamed, pimply face and what seemed to us curious views on religion: he was a Christadelphian. He had a close but pedantic knowledge of the Bible, and in spite of his enlightened views – for he did not believe in a hell – he was as literal in his interpretation of texts as any Plymouth Brother. He had discovered that Elijah did not go to heaven in a chariot of fire, as people generally thought, and in support of this he adduced Second Kings chapter ii, verse xi:

And it came to pass, as they still went on, and talked, that, behold, there appeared a chariot of fire, and horses of fire, and parted them both asunder; and Elijah went up by a whirlwind into heaven.

D. read from this that Elijah did not go up to heaven in the chariot, but in a whirlwind; but Aunt Maggie would not have it; she had been taught that Elijah went up in a chariot, and she refused to give up the chariot. For some reason I was attracted by the fancy of the whirlwind. The debate between Aunt Maggie and me went on long after D. had gone, leaving a pile of tracts behind him which my father put in the fire one day. There was a great deal of discussion among us about King David too, and how, considering all the sins he had committed, he could be a man after God's heart. My father had a soft side for David, and nodded his head in a sort of Plutarchian wonder over his character; but my mother could never quite reconcile herself to him.

There was no church in Wyre, so that on Sunday the Wyre people had to set out in their boats for Rousay across the narrow sound. Half a dozen boats would sometimes leave together on a calm summer morning, but there were many days when the weather was too rough for anyone to risk the journey. I can remember these expeditions, and Mr Pirie standing in the pulpit nodding his head, which was inclined diagonally as he followed the lines of his written sermon with his one good eye; I can see his thin hair brushed across the crown of his head to hide a small coin-like bald patch in the middle, and his straggling beard, and his brown, seamed face. He was greatly loved, though every one disapproved of his reading his sermons: people still had a strong belief in spontaneous inspiration.

We always returned from church to a good dinner of soup with a chicken, or, as we called it, more honestly, a hen, cooked in it, followed by 'spotted dog'. Now that my sailor suit has come back again I find it is associated with these Sunday dinners and the shining spoons and knives and forks laid out on the white tablecloth. During the week we did not bother much about knives and forks and tablecloths. A big plate of herring or other fish was set in the middle of the table, along with a dish of potatoes, and we simply stretched out our hands. The traditional Orkney invitation to a visitor was, 'Put in thee hand', though when a visitor appeared knives and forks were usually laid out. We hardly ever ate meat or fowl more than once a week. It was the same at all the other farms, and nobody seemed to be the worse for it. Our supper was porridge. The porridge-pot was set down in the middle of the floor, and we all sat round it with great bowls of milk and ladled the porridge into the milk.

Our diet was a curious one by town standards. We went without many necessaries, or what are considered necessaries – beef, for instance – and had a great number of luxuries which we did not know to be luxuries, such as plovers' eggs, trout, crab, and lobster: I ate so much crab and lobster as a boy that I have never been able to enjoy them since. Our staples were home-made oat bannocks and barley bannocks, butter, eggs, and home-made cheese, which we had in abundance; white bread, bought at the Wyre shop, was looked upon as a luxury. In the kitchen there was a big girnel with a sliding top; inside it was divided in two, one compartment being filled with oat-meal and the other with barley-meal. The meal had to be pressed firmly down, otherwise it would not keep. The girnel, when the top was slid aside, gave out a thick, sleepy smell which seemed to go to my head and make me drowsy. It was connected with a nightmare which I often had, in which my body seemed to swell to a great size and then slowly dwindle again, while the drowsy smell of meal filled my nostrils. It is from smell that we get our most intense realization of the solidity of things. The smell of the meal pressed tightly down in the girnel made me realize its *mass*, though I could see only its surface, which was smooth and looked quite shallow. My nightmares probably came from an apprehension of the mere bulk of life, the feeling that the world is so tightly crammed with solid bulging objects that there is not enough room for all of them: a nightmare feeling powerfully conveyed in the stories of Franz Kafka.

Our life at the Bu was virtually self-supporting. The pig, after being slaughtered each year, was cut up and salted, and the pork stored away in a barrel. I helped with the salting when I was quite small, and got a sense of pleased importance from rubbing the raw slices of meat on coarse salt strewn on a wooden board: these neat cubes did not seem to have any connexion with the butchered pig. We had fish almost as often as we wanted it, and crabs when Sutherland went to lift his creels; and Aunt Maggie was often down on the beach gathering whelks. The oat bannocks and barley bannocks, the milk, butter, cheese, and eggs, were our own produce. We sent part of the wool after the sheep-shearing down to a Border town, and it came back as blankets and cloth. We bought at the shop such things as white bread, sugar, tea, treacle, currants and raisins, and paraffin oil for the lamps.

Old Fred of the shop was a very genteel man with an accent which he had picked up in his young days while serving in a grocery store in Edinburgh. He was the only man on the island who shaved and put on a collar every day, and this set him apart from other men as a sort of priest smelling perpetually of the clean odours of tea, tobacco, and paraffin oil. He emphasized the difference by wearing a straw hat, summer and winter, both outside and inside the shop. Having seen the world, he looked down on us for our insularity, and showed that he thought his Edinburgh manners, suitable for a fine Princes Street shop, were cast away on us islanders. He was a thin, sensitive little man, terribly proper: a gentle bachelor with pernickety ways. He is long since dead.

The Lammas Market was the great yearly event. It was held in Kirkwall, but though my father and my older brothers and sisters usually went to it, I was never taken, for the journey was considered too long and tiring. On the first Monday of the market the *Fawn*, which plied between Rousay and Kirkwall, stopped a little distance out from Wyre – for there was no pier – and some one rowed out the people who wanted to go to the market. I cannot recollect my family ever setting out, but I remember clearly my brothers and sisters returning from it one year. I had bronchitis and was not allowed outside; but when they came in sight my mother let me go to the end of the house and watch them coming. I can see them still passing the corner of the ruined chapel; they were all in their best clothes; it was a still, warm summer evening. They brought presents for me, pink sweets I had never seen before, ribbed like snowdrifts, rough chunks of yellow rock, and new, dark brown, smooth sweets which I did not much care for: chocolates. I had expected a jumping-jack as well, for my mother had often described one to me which had once been in the house; but no jumping-jacks could be had at the market; they were out of fashion, and I had to put up instead with a large wooden egg, out of which a snake shot, rustling, when you opened it. I never had many toys, and never got much genuine satisfaction from them: the enjoyment was conscious make-believe with an undercurrent of disappointment: I always expected every toy to do more than it could do.

We had very few visitors in Wyre, for the island was difficult to reach except in perfectly calm weather. Mr Pirie sometimes came across from Rousay to call on his parishioners or to hold a prayer meeting in the school. An auctioneer from Kirkwall, a jolly young man in a blue serge suit, came one wet, cold afternoon – he had some business at another farm – and gave me a sandwich, the first I had ever seen: he seemed to have a great number of them in his pockets. And a queer man in a soft, grey suit with a very high, stiff collar knocked at our door one summer evening. He spoke in a shrill voice with a thin, whining accent; he was extravagantly polite and amiable; but his face was dead white and jumped about so much as he chattered and giggled that I hid behind my father and peeped out at him from there. We did not know what to make of him, but after he had left Sutherland said that he was 'moonstruck' – the adjective still used at that time in Orkney to describe lunatics. Rich young men who were not in their right minds were often sent to farms in remote islands then; a good number of them reached Orkney, and the Orkney people had a name for them, calling them 'feeders', since they ate without doing any work. The poor man who had called on us and tried to amuse us was a 'feeder' kept by a Rousay farmer who, wanting to give him a change, had rowed him across to Wyre to wander about there, and presently rowed him back again.

Our greatest friends in Wyre were the Ritches of the Haa, a

handsome family with a sense of fun, and gentle manners. John Ritch, the father, was my father's closest friend; they had been next-door neighbours in Deerness, and in Wyre they got farms next to each other again. John Ritch was a skilled tailor and a fine fiddler as well as a farmer. He was one of the most handsome men I have ever seen, tall and straight, with a fine solid brow and nose and a square trimmed beard; he was more particular about his appearance than most farmers, and had a dignified jocosity which quite beguiled us. There was a sort of feud between him and Sutherland, who had no dignity, and whenever John Ritch came to our house Sutherland would tell one thundering lie after another, hoping to annoy him. But John Ritch, without losing his temper, would say gravely, 'Thu kens in thee conscience, Sutherland, that thu's telling a lee.' And Sutherland would answer brazenly, 'And *I* ken in *me* conscience that I'm *no* telling a lee.' This dialogue would go on for a long time, while the rest of us looked on as at a play.

The language we spoke was a mixture of Norse, Scots, and Irish. The second person singular was in full working order, and we used it as it is used in French and German, addressing our friends as 'thu' and 'thee' and strangers and official personages as 'you'; we had a sure sense of the distinction and were never at a loss. The men spoke for the most part in a slow, deliberate voice, but some of the women could rattle on at a great rate in the soft sing-song lilt of the islands, which has remained unchanged for over a thousand years. For the Orkney people, or the Norse part of them, came more than that length of time ago from two little valleys in the south of Norway, and the inflection of their voices is still the same as that of the present inhabitants of these valleys, having remained unchanged while the whole fabric of speech was transformed. It is a soft and musical inflection, slightly melancholy, but companionable, the voice of people who are accustomed to hours of talking in the long winter evenings and do not feel they need to hurry: a splendid voice for telling stories in. It still keeps some of the quality of a chant, and I feel that in its early stages a language is always chanted, since it is new enough still to be cherished as an almost miraculous thing. The strangeness fades, and language becomes workable and common-place.

The idiom of the Orkney language has some fine old inversions and a few archaic words like 'moonstruck' and 'phial' and 'sib'. 'Tells thu me yon?' ('Tell you me that?') is the habitual order. 'That wad I no' is an emphatic 'I wouldn't think of such a thing.' The syntactical feeling is much stronger than in ordinary urban or educated speech, and has more resemblance to that of the seventeenth century. These traditional inversions, which give such an exact value to the order of words in a sentence, have been ironed out by the Educational System, and very few of them remain now. Most of the local poets who appear in Orkney write in an English laboriously learned from the grammar books; but I except from this generalization two very fine poets, Robert Rendall and George Brown. The islands produce a terrible number of professors. But simple, uneducated people here and there still speak a beautiful language and know where to set a word in a sentence.

I cannot say how much my idea of a good life was influenced by my early upbringing, but it seems to me that the life of the little island of Wyre was a good one, and that its sins were mere sins of the flesh, which are excusable, and not sins of the spirit. The farmers did not know ambition and the petty torments of ambition; they did not realize what competition was, though they lived at the end of Queen Victoria's reign; they helped one another with their work when help was required, following the old usage; they had a culture made up of legend, folk-song, and the poetry and prose of the Bible; they had customs which sanctioned their instinctive feelings for the earth; their life was an order, and a good order. So that when my father and mother left Orkney for Glasgow when I was fourteen, we were plunged out of order into chaos. We did not know it at the time, and I did not realize it for many years after I had left Glasgow. My father and mother and two of my brothers died in Glasgow within two years of one another. Four members of our family died there within two years. That is a measure of the violence of the change.

I have only a vague memory of our year at Helye, at the end of which we left Wyre for a farm on the mainland near Kirkwall. My attack of terrified guilt came on me during that year; but except for it all I can remember is that I never liked Helye as well as the Bu, which was a kindly house.

For many years after leaving Wyre I never dreamed about it once; it was as if that part of my life had been forgotten. My first dream of it came twenty-five years later, when I was being psychoanalysed in London. I dreamed that I was standing at the bow of a boat; it was early morning, and the sky and the sea were milk-white. The ship went on with a rustling motion, and cut more deeply into the ever-deepening round of the horizon. A spire rose above the rim of the sea, and at once, as the ship rushed smoothly on, I could see the little streets, the prickly weeds growing out of the walls, the tangle dripping from the pier. The houses opened out, melted and ran together; in a moment I would be there; but then I saw that this was not the town I knew, and that the people walking about the streets were strangers. Then, the ship clean gone, I was wandering along the top of a high, craggy coast. Far beneath me the sea snarled in the caves, which like marine monsters gnashed at it and spat it out again; opposite, across the boiling strait, so near that I felt I could touch it, was Rousay with its towering black mountain. I had never thought that the coast of Wyre was so wild and rocky, and even as this thought formed in my mind the isle grew tamer, grew quite flat, and I was walking along a brown path level with the sea, picking great, light, violet-hued, crown-shaped flowers which withered at once in my hands. I came to a little chapel or shrine on the shore. On one wall a brown clay image was hanging: a weatherbeaten image of an old woman naked to the waist, with sun-burned, wrinkled dugs. I went up to the image, and as if I were fulfilling some ritual pressed one of the nipples with my finger. A trembling flowed over the figure, and, like a wave running across another in counter-motion, the texture changed; the clay quivered and rippled with life, all the marks of age vanishing in that transparent flood; the breasts shone smooth and round, and rose and fell with living breath. At the same time in the centre of my breast I felt a hot, tingling fire, and I knew that a yellow sun was blazing there, and with its beams, which filled my body with light and soft power, was raising the image from the dead. The figure came down from the wall, a dark brown girl, and stood beside me. That is all I remember about the dream, which ended before I reached the Bu, though I felt a great longing to return there. It was as if the dream, having set out to take me back to that house which I loved so much, were offering me something else instead, reanimating another image of whose existence I did not know.

I had a dream later of the Bu itself, though again everything was strangely transfigured and transposed. I was walking up a little winding road; I had been away for a long time, and now, an old man, I had returned. Great trees stood round the house, their foliage darker and thicker than any I had ever seen, the leaves hanging like dark green tongues one over the other in a motionless security which no wind could reach. The walls appeared behind them, thick walls so rounded and softened by time that no jutting angle or corner remained: in the middle was a great wooden gate like the gate of an old castle. Above the house rose a low grey sky, a particular sky arched over it alone: there was nothing but the great walls, the dark trees, and the low, round sky. I stood and looked at the house, filled with quiet expectation, but I did not go in.

Another dream also points back to Wyre, but even less directly than these two: I set it down to show how early impressions may grow and take on the form of myth. One day when I was about five or six my Aunt Maggie pointed at a gleaming grey bird standing on the farther edge of the pond below the house, and cried, 'Look, there's a heron!' As she pointed the heron rose in the air and effortlessly flew away on its wide-spread wings. I was filled with fear and wonder at the slow winging of the great bird, and its very name, the 'heron', seemed to have a strange significance. In the dream I was walking with some people in the country, when I saw a shining grey bird in a field. I turned and said in an awed voice, 'It's a heron.' We went towards it, but as we came nearer it spread its tail like a peacock, so that we could see nothing else. As the tail grew I saw that it was not round, but square, an impenetrable grey hedge of feathers; and at once I knew that its body was not a bird's body now, but an animal's, and that behind that gleaming hedge it was walking away from us on four feet padded like a leopard's or a tiger's. Then, confronting it in the field, there appeared an ancient, dirty, earth-coloured animal with a head like that of an old sheep or a mangy dog. Its eyes were soft and brown; it was alone against the splendid-tailed beast; yet it stood its ground and prepared to fight the danger coming towards it, whether that was death or merely humiliation and pain. From their look I could see that the two animals knew each other, that they had fought a countless number of times and after this battle would fight again, that each meeting would be the first meeting, and that the dark, patient animal would always be defeated, and the bright, fierce animal would always win. I did not see the fight, but I knew it would be ruthless and shameful, with a meaning of some kind perhaps, but no comfort.

Dresden and Hellerau

[The earlier chapters of *An Autobiography* were written in the late thirties. 'Since then there has been a great war and a succession of revolutions; the world has been divided into two hostile camps; and our concern has ceased to be the community or country we live in, and has become the single, disunited world . . . This world was set going when we began to make nature serve us, hoping that we should eventually reach a stage where we would not have to adapt ourselves at all: machinery would save the trouble. We did not foresee that the machinery would grow into a great impersonal power . . . This terrible impersonality is the mark of the last twenty or thirty years.']

This awareness of the direction in which the world is moving, which came to me so belatedly, casts doubt on my memory of these years in the early 'twenties when my wife and I lived in Dresden and Hellerau. Yet they still seem to me among the happiest of my life. We lived by ourselves in a town pleasantly strange. Everything seemed good, the houses, the streets, the people, because we were disposed to find them so. The Saxons are not a handsome race, but I was not looking for beauty, and when I encountered it in some chance face it was so unusual that it surprised me, and awoke a sense almost of alarm. There was so much of life which I had not accepted and felt the need to accept, that what I wanted now was the ordinary as the reassuring, given substance of life – round faces and blank blue eyes and comfortable bodies – and here they were in plenty, more consoling than any more carefully finished sketch of the human form could have been. These people were like a race still in the making, and quite content to be so, affirming without knowing it that the material out of which mankind is shaped has a simple natural virtue. When we went out for our mid-day meal at some nearby restaurant and saw Saxons converging upon it with greetings of 'Guten Appetit' or 'Mahlzeit', the simplicity of that salutation, that blessing on the stomach and its doings, though the mere observance of a convention, moved us genuinely. It confirmed and blessed the rite of eating.

In Dresden we lived in an agreeable, silent vacuum, except for the talk of our garrulous landlady Frau Mütze, who was always asking us to get a nice English husband for her pretty daughter. Now and then we met John Holms and his wife, who had turned up shortly after our arrival. We lodged on the top floor of a large insurance building in the Old Town, and looked down on a square and beyond it, through a fringe of trees, at the Elbe. Except for the time I spent in writing my articles for the American *Freeman*, on which we lived, we had our days to ourselves. We employed them in learning German, and reading German poetry, and seeing the sights, and visiting cabarets, and attending concerts with the Holmses. The Germans whom we met were friendly, perhaps all the more so because they could practise their English, after long disuse, on us as accommodating patients. They did not show any bitterness at the defeat of their country, or any envy at our good fortune in being on the winning side. All this seemed now in a sense pointless, and it was assumed that they and we were above such considerations. I think that at that time the Germans sincerely wished to be reconciled with the world.

The Dresden we knew then, that spacious, handsome city, has since been destroyed in a war of which we never dreamt. Hitler was already collecting a small group around him in Munich, but in Dresden and Hellerau we never heard his name or knew that he existed. We knew nothing either, after living some months in the town, of the many families ruined by the war and the inflation: old people whose life-savings had disappeared as through a hole in a sack; comfortable families reduced to bewildered poverty. We became aware of these things only a year or so after we went to Hellerau. There, as we came to know almost everyone in the little community, we realized the difficulty they had in dealing with each day as it rose. But Dresden looked ambiguously prosperous; the people were well-dressed, the shops well-stocked, the places of entertainment filled: not a sign of ruin hiding in its respectable burrows.

We lived there in ignorance, not looking ahead. In spring we watched the sweet-smelling lime blossom coming out on the trees bordering the streets, and in summer spent a great deal of time on the banks of the river, sun-bathing among the seal-like Saxons whose skin was tanned to a Red Indian brown: a pleasant, vacant life without a trace of boredom, for everything round us was strange. My wife began a play, and I attempted one or two poems, with indifferent success. Holms tried to make up his mind whether Wagner compared with Beethoven could be called a great man, and whether love satisfied or love unfulfilled was the better inspiration for the artist, Wagner standing for the first and Beethoven for the second. He spoke of a long poem he had in mind on the metamorphoses of the animals, in which the various species would be shown emerging pictorially in the course of a long magical process, by an enormous speeding up and simplification of time. But the lethargy which weighed upon him did not lift long enough for him even to start. To begin, to find a fulcrum for the lever which would raise him to the point he would be at, was the problem that he was never able to solve.

One autumn evening, as we were waiting at a tram stop, we ran against A. S. Neill, who was an old friend of my wife. He told us that he had started an international school at Hellerau and begged her to come out there and help him. After thinking it over for a few days she agreed, and a fortnight later we moved to the house of Frau Doktor Neustätter, five minutes' walk from the school. She was an Australian married to a Bavarian doctor who worked in the Ministry of Health in Dresden. She helped Neill with his work.

The people we knew in Hellerau made up a small community gathered round an euryhthmic school which Jacques Dalcroze had built there and had forsaken after the war. It was a spacious building, with a theatre and lecture rooms and dancing-halls and tennis courts. The central part was now used as a school of dancing, one of the wings housed Neill's international school, and the other a school for the Hellerau children. We all had our mid-day meal each day in the Schulheim. The dancing students, mostly young women, were drawn from most of the countries in Europe; the common language was German. My wife taught in Neill's school every morning. The students were often in Frau Neustätter's hospitable house in the evenings, and we came to know them all.

All this was thirty years ago, and with one half of my mind I can look at it historically, while the other half still sees it as I saw it then, wrapped in its own illusions. We lived, it seems to me now, in a climate of 'new ideas', and looked forward to a 'new life' which would be brought about by the simple exercise of freedom, a freedom such as had never been formulated before in any terms, since it too was new. We were, or thought we were, without 'prejudices'. We 'accepted' everything, no matter what it might be. We were interested in psychoanalysis, not as a scientific method but as a magical process which would deliver us from our inhibitions and leave us with a freedom all the dearer because it was beyond our imagining. We did not know that the climate in which we lived was already growing colder, or if we did we took care to keep it at its level of liberal warmth. While the inflation was spreading around us like a dry rot, we thought only of a potentiality which would, almost without our lifting a finger, painlessly realize itself and deposit us in a new existence. Our desire for that new state, which was so clearly good since it was all freedom, seemed to give us a foretaste of it. To dream, and to dream 'scientifically', of such things as techniques triumphantly employed, prejudices dispelled, complexes dissolved, was to us a sort of activity which could achieve its end only by a wise suspension of all effort. A life without an obstacle, activity without endeavour, desires which would spontaneously exhale into universal freedom: that was our dream. Actually our desires did not behave in this way, nor indeed, with the sensible part of our minds, did we expect it; in our conduct we observed the usual conventions without noticing it, and were annoyed when anyone violated them, for it caused, to our surprise, all sorts of inconveniences. We felt free without practising freedom; we merely talked; and to talk freely gives an illusion of freedom hardly to be distinguished, except by an intellectual effort, from the reality. We discussed everything.

How much I was immersed in that atmosphere I cannot say, perhaps more than I realized. Reading some of my articles for the *Freeman* written about that time, I see that I was very little concerned with the truth of what I said; I was simply letting my mind range freely among 'ideas', as if that were a sufficient end in itself. I had started the habit in Glasgow, where ideas were so scarce that any, good or bad, was a treasure to be prized. I had afterwards come under the influence of Orage, the most intelligent merchant of ideas of his time. But in Hellerau my imagination was beginning to waken after a long sleep, and the perceptions it promised were so much more real than those with which I had been trifling, that these no longer excited me. Some of them vanished altogether and were as if they had never been; others transmuted themselves into imaginative forms, particularly those which touched the ideas of innocence and reconciliation: Eden and the millennial vision of which I had dreamt as a child. The atmosphere in which our little community lived, with its affirmation of a freedom of mere wish and thought, had indeed in it something which faintly evoked the image of Eden and the prophecy of the time when the lion would lie down with the lamb: a nonsensical Eden, no doubt, and a sentimental lion and lamb, but touching as things genuinely felt. My image of Eden was associated with these naturally good and charming people, and the innocence with which they used their supposed freedom. They have been scattered long since to their own countries or exiled to others; they have grown into the real world, and the life they lived in Hellerau, which they could not have continued to live in any case after a certain age, has quite disappeared from the world. Some of them probably died in the gas chambers, and among them one or two who had such a genius for happiness that I still cannot imagine them as being anything but happy.

This provincial dream was fostered by its surroundings. Hellerau – I had better speak of it in the past tense, for the war may have destroyed it as it has destroyed Dresden – was a little garden city, the first of its kind, and the model, I believe, of the English ones. It had been originally intended for craftsmen, and was pleasantly secluded among sweetbrier hedges and in the midst of pine woods. The small population when we went there were no longer chiefly craftsmen; government officials from Dresden and faddists of all kinds had settled in the place. But all of them had acquired a distinct character which would not have been found in any other small German town, a certain amenity and mazed tolerance. They met in the evenings at a little tavern on the edge of a pine wood to drink and converse or, in summer, to dance outside in the courtyard.

In other parts of Germany, particularly in the large cities, the freedom we amateurishly cultivated had been pushed far beyond any bounds we could imagine. It was the age of Expressionism and the New Objectivity. The Expressionists carried freedom to a point where it lost all meaning and became an elaborate torment. They were driven by a need to pour out the last dirty dregs of the mind, as if it were a duty to appal themselves and their readers; one could hear in their works the last hysterical retchings, perhaps the death-rattle of freedom. The New Objectivity set out to describe things as they were, and it too was involved in the nightmare, for the state of the large cities was as horrible as the visions of the Expressionists. But in Hellerau we did not know of that terrible and apparently real freedom which assumed that since everything was possible everything was allowable; and we could continue our dream.

The German landscape, as I have said, helped to foster it. There was something in the appearance of the woods which seemed to invite nature-worship, and from nature-worship to worship of our own nature, which we were modestly practising, was an easy step. The trees solicited us to be natural, since they were natural, to be young, since they renewed their youth every year, to be child-like, since we could easily feel as we wandered among them that we were children of nature. The German poetry we read added to this mild enchantment. The poems of childhood in particular, so numerous and so unlike those of Vaughan and Traherne – poems of natural not of heavenly innocence – softly persuaded us that it was sweet not to grow up.

What I am trying to describe is an enchantment. It was so strong that it could transmute and use for its ends the most recalcitrant material, such as the ideas of Freud. The child of nature, the companion of the woods and streams, would enter into a still more perfect communion with them when he had resolved his complexes.

The worship of nature was a powerful cult in Germany in these years after the war. There were a few nature and self-worshippers in Hellerau: I remember a thin dusky man who always seemed to be working in his garden, clad in nothing but a loin-cloth, eye-glasses and a wrist watch, and always with the serious air of one making an important, if misunderstood, demonstration. The self-worship took more elaborate forms. As I sat one evening in Frau Neustätter's garden I saw a tall handsome man in flowing robes, a fillet round his head, passing majestically with a beautiful subservient young woman on either side. I never saw him again, and hardly know whether he was a visiting prophet or an apparition. But in the weekends the simple-lifers, the direct worshippers of nature, came out from Dresden and crowded in the woods. They called themselves the Wandervögel; they neither smoked nor drank; instead they carried guitars, and sang German songs, and kindled ritual fires, and slept, young men and women together, in the woods. The war had made them poor and wakened in them a need to be with harmless unwarlike things like trees and streams, and to move freely through peaceful spaces. Most of them, I have been told, were carried away later by the gospel of Hitler. They had nothing but simplicity and a belief that smoking and drinking were evil to protect them against him.

There were, outside the Schulheim, some people with a different philosophy of life. I met one day a stiffly polite, stiffly superior, apparently rich young man who had just returned from a visit to the circle in which Stefan George, the poet, passed his life. He told me that George was the only hope for Germany, and that I should not be distracted by the simple antics of the Wandervögel. (The Wandervögel eventually turned out to be more powerful than the poet.) I had not read George at that time and did not know that he was a great poet in spite of his curious ideas. On the young man's advice I bought a book on him by Gundolf, a member of the circle, and was repelled by its mixture of superciliousness and reverence, in which the reverence was so plainly based on the superciliousness. George was a man of proud spirit, with a devotion to the art of poetry unique in Germany in his time; but he could follow it only in seclusion, and he had been imprisoned for a long time within the circle he had summoned to guard him: it cut him off from life. When he escaped from it into his earlier memories he could still be a great poet; as it was, he went on shaping himself in his self-imposed privacy until he became incapable of shaping experience. It was greatly to his honour that, when the Nazis began to court him as one who had also dreamt a dream of a Third Empire, he would have nothing to do with them. He went into exile and before his death gave orders that he should be buried with his face turned away from Germany. I mention him because at the time he had power over a small but influential group of intellectuals.

In a sort of friendly detachment there lived in Hellerau an impoverished Junker, Ivo von Lucken. He had lost all he had in the inflation and lived in a little basement room in the Schulheim which he never let anyone enter, I think because of its extreme bareness. He gave lessons in Spanish and was paid by his students, at his own request, in parcels of food, pounds of rice, pats of butter. He was a high-nosed, hawk-faced man of an extraordinary sweetness and courtesy, so innocently simple that he would tell the most embarrassingly absurd stories against himself; most of them were about his time in the army during the war, when he never seemed to have carried out an order rightly, or managed to make his uniform fit him. As he spoke of these things a look of surprise would settle on his face, for he could never account for the strange difficulties that beset him during that time. He was interested in poetry and goodness, not at all in politics. He knew most of the living German poets and had himself written poetry of which nobody seems to have taken any notice. But that did not in the least disturb him; his devotion to the poetry of others was too great, and his own vanity too small. Although he had lost all his money and lived in great poverty, I never heard him make any complaint. He was tubercular, and his lodging in the basement must have been very bad for his health; but to him this predicament was simply a fact to be adapted to his style of life – a style created out of a complete lack of pettiness and a refusal to recognize the existence of time. My wife and I often tried to wile him to have a meal with us, but he would never admit to himself that he had any need of one, and only once or twice did he consent, with an air of elaborate carelessness, and then, as a point of private honour, would eat very little. He had one desire, which he often came back to, though with the detachment of one speaking of a dream: he wanted to go to Spain. It is unlikely that he ever had his wish. When I think of all the people I knew in Hellerau, I feel that he for one could never have gone across to the Nazis: his innocence would have saved him. Indeed he lived with Hölderlin more than with any living man, and he was more pleased when he succeeded in making me begin to understand that great poet than when he got a parcel of food from his students. I cannot remember that he had any 'views'; I think he had only devotions. Of all the people in Hellerau he was the poorest, but also possibly the happiest.

I have often wondered how many of the people I knew then, and which among them, went over to the Nazis ten years later, when Hitler came to power. I know of two who stood out: one, a Gentile, was shot by the Nazis; the other, a Jew, was shot a decade later by the Russians when they occupied Dresden.

We left Hellerau in 1923, when the inflation was making life intolerable and the guilt of appearing responsible for it, however indirectly, was more than we could face. I remember the days of mourning, mourning rather than bitterness, when news came that the French had sent 'black' troops into the Ruhr. The mourning in a little turned sour as the inflation made life impossible. A year or so after we left, when a Communist majority came to power in Saxony, Neill had to give up his school and move what was left of it to Austria. By then people had become so desperate that they were willing to listen to Hitler or Thaelmann or anybody. We tried to salve our consciences in the last few months by taking our German friends in relays to Dresden for a good meal. But we felt at last that we had no right to be in the country.

In the year and a half before things worsened I was beginning to write poetry. I had no training; I was too old to submit myself to contemporary influences; and I had acquired in Scotland a deference towards ideas which made my entrance into poetry difficult. Though my imagination had begun to work I had no technique by which I could give expression to it. There were the rhythms of English poetry on the one hand, the images in my mind on the other. All I could do at the start was to force the one, creaking and complaining, into the mould of the other. I have come to realize since then that Pound and Eliot were wise in regarding the first stages in the writing of poetry as a sort of apprenticeship, to be learned like any other. I know now what Eliot means when he says that Dante is the best model for a contemporary poet. But I did not know then, nor did I even like Eliot's poetry: it took me several years to recognize its great virtues. I had caught from John Holms a devotion for Wordsworth, but Wordsworth is not a poet to be imitated, and if the thought had occurred to me then, I would have regarded it as presumption. I began to write poetry simply because what I wanted to say could not have gone properly into prose. I wanted so much to say it that I had no thought left to study the form in which alone it could be said.

I certainly knew far too little about myself; yet I feel now that, in spite of the troubles brought about by my ignorance, I was more fortunate than the young poet (I was not even young) who knows too much or thinks he knows too much about poetry, and can solve with ease the technical problems which I could not solve at all. To think of poetry like this makes it a simple and business-like, and may make it almost a clever thing. I wrote in baffling ignorance, blundering and perpetually making mistakes. I must have been influenced by something, since we all are, but when I try to find out what it was that influenced me, I can only think of the years of childhood which I spent on my father's farm in the little island of Wyre in Orkney, and the beauty I apprehended then, before I knew there was beauty. These years had come alive, after being forgotten for so long, and when I wrote about horses they were my father's plough-horses as I saw them when I was four or five; and a poem on Achilles pursuing Hector round the walls of Troy was really a resuscitation of the afternoon when I ran away, in real terror, from another boy as I returned from school. The bare landscape of the little island became, without my knowing it, a universal landscape over which Abraham and Moses and Achilles and Ulysses and Tristram and all sorts of pilgrims passed; and Troy was associated with the Castle, a mere green mound, near my father's house.

I do not know whether in others the impressions of the first seven years of their lives remain so vivid and lasting, or if it is good that they should. In any case we need a symbolical stage on which the drama of human life can play itself out for us, and I doubt whether we have the liberty to choose it. The little island was not too big for a child to see in it an image of life; land and sea and sky, good and evil, happiness and grief, life and death discovered themselves to me there; and the landscape was so simple that it made these things simple too. In his youth my father had known witches in the island of Sanday, from which he came, and often spoke of them. My Aunt Maggie used to tell a story of a cruel mother who starved her little daughter by baking for her every day a stone covered with a thin layer of dough, and made her sleep in damp sheets so that she might fall ill and die. Aunt Maggie would recite the lugubrious little song the child sang to herself:

> I wiss me dame was hame
> And I had pickéd me stane,
> I wiss me sheet was weet
> And I laid doon tae sleep.

I listened entranced to this story, and fitted its cruelty unreflectingly into my picture, never doubting that it had a right to be there. The witches and the cruel mother, the honest ploughman and the good minister, had an equal and justified place in my world. In recollecting these years in Wyre I recovered an image of life more complete than I had known in all the years between.

This naïve acceptance lasted for a year or two after we left Wyre and my father moved to the farm of Garth, some four miles from Kirkwall. I was returning from the Kirkwall Burgh School one summer afternoon when I caught up with a cart driven by a neighbouring farmer. He invited me to climb in at the back, and I found myself beside a very pale young man who smiled to me and then stared at something which he alone seemed to see; for he never looked at the fields and the distant sea where so many things were happening. The farmer glanced round and said, 'This is my son, home from Leith.' Then he turned away again and nothing more was said until I got off at the end of the path that led to our house. When I got there I told my mother about the young man; she looked grave and made no reply; but later in the evening I heard her telling my father about the neighbour's son and saying that he had 'come home to die'. The words were simple and yet strange, and dying became a sad and deliberate act which could be accomplished only in its own place, and for which careful provision had to be made. I learned later that the young man had 'fallen into a decline' as it was still called in Orkney, and that he was in the last stages of it.

A few weeks later, standing at the end of the house, I watched the funeral procession moving along the distant road. There were six men in front carrying the coffin on their shoulders, and behind them a long line of men in black clothes. Presently they reached the edge of a hill and one by one disappeared. But I stood for a long time afterwards looking at the white empty road, the hills and the sea, and what thoughts were in my mind then I shall never know; they were certainly tinged with sadness, but at the same time suffused with wonder and a simple acceptance of wonder. The fields were empty out of respect to the dead. It was a calm bright summer day and the hills and the sea hung suspended in light and peace.

These distant memories returned to me in Hellerau, but I scarcely knew that my image of the world had changed. I went on writing a poetry of symbols drawn from memory without realizing that I was doing so. I continued to do this for ten years before I became aware of it, and then only when it was pointed out. I fancy that the longer a poet writes the better he knows what he is doing: it is an advantage and a danger. An advantage, for the task of a poet is to make his imaginative world clear to himself. A danger, for that world in becoming clear may grow hard and shallow and obscure the mystery which it once embodied. We do not know enough about such things.

We left Hellerau in the spring of 1923 for a little town in Italy where Holms and his wife had rented a lodge which they wished us to share, as it was too expensive for them.

Glasgow

I

. . . I lived in Glasgow for fifteen years, and the only way in which I can give any picture of it is by digging into a whole series of impressions, old and new, and one buried beneath another. The advantage of this method is that it will show Glasgow from a number of sides; the disadvantage is that I shall have to forgo objective observation; but I could not have avoided that in any case. This will make my picture of Glasgow more detailed than that of any other city I shall write about; but that again is as it should be, for Glasgow is in every way the most important city in modern Scotland, since it is an epitome of the virtues and the vices of the industrial regions, which comprise the majority of the population. A description of Scotland which did not put Glasgow in the centre of the picture would not be a description of Scotland at all.

Yet at the same time Glasgow is not a typically Scottish town; the worst of the many evils with which it festers were not born of the soil on which it stands or of the people who live in it – a mixed population of Lowlanders, Highlanders, and Irish – but of Industrialism; and in writing about it I shall be writing about a particular area of modern civilization which is independent of national boundaries, and can be found in England, Germany, Poland, Czechoslovakia and most other countries as well as on the banks of the Clyde. This No Man's Land of civilization comprises in Scotland an area which, though not very large in extent, is very densely populated. In one way it may be said that this area *is* modern Scotland, since it is the most active and vital part of Scotland as well as the most populous; the proof of its vitality being that it influences rural Scotland in all sorts of ways, while rural Scotland has no effective influence on it. But from another point of view one may say that it is not Scotland at all, or not

Scotland in particular, since it is merely one of the expressions of Industrialism, and Industrialism operates by laws which do not recognize nationality. To say that is to say that Scotland is in the same position as most other European countries, except those which are still mainly agricultural. One part of its life is traditional and closely bound to the soil; another part is modern and has no immediate bond with the soil. Glasgow is consequently far more like Manchester than like Edinburgh. It is more like a manufacturing town anywhere in Europe than like a Scottish town which has preserved the old traditions of life. If the picture is sordid, then, the reader should remember this.

The spectre of Industrialism has kept on appearing in this book, and its appearance may possibly give the impression that I look upon Industrialism as completely evil, and a thing that should be speedily abolished, so that everybody might return to a more simple and healthy way of life. As I shall have a great deal more to say about Industrialism in this chapter, I should state my attitude to it as clearly as possible now. By Industrialism I mean the distinctively modern form of capitalist production and exchange which was set going over a century ago by a generally sanctioned greed such as the world had never seen before, called competition, and went on perpetuating itself in security once that greed had achieved the logical infallibility of a law. In working itself out, this process took no regard of human life, unless when it was compelled to do so; it devastated whole tracts of the country-side, and sucked the life and youth out of the rest; it huddled up as quickly and cheaply as it could great deserts of towns, quite unsuitable for human habitation; and it set its mark on several generations of the men, women and children by whose work it lived, in shrunken bodies and trivial or embittered minds. In return for this it increased vastly the total wealth of the world, and raised considerably the general standard of comfort in those countries where it prevailed. If Industrialism were suddenly to stop now, and we had to judge it by its past history, it would appear a mad dream, without justification. But a historical process incarnated in the flesh and blood of whole peoples cannot stop until it has worked itself out. Nor

146

can it be stopped from outside by deliberate reason or goodwill, and another and apparently better system substituted for it. It can at most be directed towards its natural desirable end, and the conditions for the realization of that aim are present, it seems to an increasing number of people, in our time. Industrialism as at present managed is breaking down under the weight of the problems it has created without solving, and there is a growing belief among all classes of people that it must be consciously controlled if disaster is to be avoided, and the potential good in the system realized. The logical end of Industrialism is a state of general wealth and leisure. The American technologists have proved that that is theoretically possible, and Major Douglas, in his programme of Social Credit, has outlined a way of realizing it peacefully. Socialist and Communist writers of all shades base their doctrines of social improvement on the same assumption – that is, that Industrialism, or the system of modern capitalist production, can be so used that it will benefit everybody, and turn from a curse into a blessing. Industrialism is therefore a thing which it would be an act of madness to discard in favour of a simple agricultural ideal of society, if that were possible. It is our chief earnest of the future, and the whole problem of the future centres in it. That is another reason why industrial Scotland is more important than the rest of Scotland. The main battle of the present is being fought out in it.

If, then, I paint a dark picture of Industrialism in the succeeding chapters, it is simply in the hope that the evils of present-day Industrialism may be realized and the necessity for taking it in hand brought home as vividly as possible to the reader. And if, in my description of the rural community of the Orkneys, which will come later, the colours will be pleasing, that it partly because they are actually so, but mainly because I wish to deepen the darkness of my picture of industrial Glasgow by contrasting with it a normal traditional mode of existence. The future, whatever it may be, will not be like the small-holding Belloc and Chesterton paradise of Orkney. Life there is far more harmonious and satisfying, it is true, than in any other place I found in my journey. It confirms Belloc's and

Chesterton's claim that Distributism is a humanly desirable economic system. But for its realization that system requires special conditions; these conditions are present in Orkney: they are not present in Glasgow or Dundee or Manchester. Nor is it conceivable that they will ever be.

With this explanation I can now go on to give my impressions of Glasgow, some old and some new, and mostly, I am afraid, painful.

II

I shall begin with my earliest impressions of Glasgow, for they are still the most vivid and reproduce, I imagine, the first instinctive response to Industrialism of anyone who has been brought up quite beyond reach of it. Later in life we become used to things which shocked us at first, and it is impossible for an industrial town-dweller born in an industrial town to realize the full squalor of his surroundings; he could not live in them if he did, for there is in everyone a necessity to form an attachment to the patch of earth and stone around him. Yet that necessity signifies nothing more than a fundamental human impulse which has existed ever since man settled down in one place and made a home and friends; it is no argument for the goodness of any place; even some slum-dwellers have it. As I continued to live in Glasgow I therefore acquired a liking for it, and that very much influenced my later impressions of it, making me reject, partly out of gratitude, partly out of an unconscious desire to spare my own feelings, the more unpleasant ones. I shall try, for the sake of truth, to correct that bias now.

But at the beginning, when I arrived in Glasgow straight from Orkney, I had no self-protective apparatus for selecting my impressions, and was stunned by a succession of sights which I frantically strove not to see. The main problem which puzzled me at that time was how all these people could live in such places without feeling ashamed. The street my family lived in was in a respectable suburb on the South Side. Most of the people in it were better-paid clerks, shopkeepers, foremen, buyers, commercial travellers: a respectable church-going lot intent on making money and rising, as the saying goes, in the world. They lived in what seemed to me comfort: that is, they had several rooms in their houses, containing sofas, arm-chairs, pianos, pictures and knick-knacks of all kinds. When they went out they were well-dressed. But the streets they walked through, the sky above them, the ground beneath their feet, the house-walls on either side of them were so squalid (even in a respectable suburb) that for a long time I could not reconcile the personal neatness and cleanliness of these people with the surrounding filth, and attributed even to the most self-satisfied among them a feeling of shame which they did not possess at all (though I am convinced that it exists as a customary suppression in most respectable people who live in places like Glasgow). They gave me somewhat the same feeling as I would have if I were told that a handsome, groomed and curled, socially popular, top-hatted, frock-coated pillar of business and the Church lived in a lavatory. After I had been in Glasgow for a few years I lost this feeling, but I still think it was natural. For one of the distinguishing marks of Industrialism is the permanent contrast between the people who live amidst it, if they are sensitive in any degree or even wish to exist in decency, and all their surroundings. As these people cease to feel the painfulness of this contrast – and they are bound to do so – they inevitably become insensitive; and I think one may assert without being unfair that the middle- and upper-classes of towns like Glasgow, where dirt and squalor are an inseparable and normal part of one's life, even if one has a bath where one can wash them off, or a commodious house where one can forget them, have a sort of comfortable insensitiveness which cannot be found in any other class or in any other place. There may be many intelligent and humane men and women in these classes, but somewhere or other they are blunted or dead; they have blind-spots as big as a door: the door of their office or of their house. They cannot help that; it is not their fault, but the fault of a system which forces them to gather money out of the dirt. But the self-protective need to ignore this involves a deliberate blunting of one whole area of their sensibility.

This applied, I found, not only to the very rich, but to all classes of individuals in Glasgow whose main ideal was respectability or rising in the world. In such people the wish to get on was not merely a natural desire, but the chief article in an exalted mystical faith, an orthodoxy which it would have been mere vicious perversity or worse not to subscribe to. Inherited Calvinism was at the bottom of their contemptuous reprobation of anyone who, out of weakness or amiability or scruple, refrained from striving to his utmost to make money; for their attitude to such people was indistinguishable from that of the elect to the damned a century before. The word 'success' had accordingly the same mystical inviolability to them as the word 'service' has since taken on among Rotarians: and even then the two words had established an *entente* among the young, striving men who attended such institutions as the YMCA, where business and religion had always gone hand in hand. I can still remember (I was about eighteen at the time) one of the most blatant of these young strivers pouring out his heart to me as we walked to our work one morning through Eglinton Street, a long and dreary slum. He began by asking me what I thought was the greatest thing in the world, and when I could not think of a reply, he exclaimed: '*I* think it's service!' I had no idea what service meant then, for the Rotarians had not been heard of, and we had an argument which I have forgotten; but in that fantastic conversation I can see the beginning of the process by which personal greed has been turned, in the years since, into the very quintessence of altruism. It is clear that they were already associated, and that is no doubt why success was talked of with such respect.

I have referred back this worship of success to Calvin, and I think he was largely responsible for it; but it was sanctified also by an orthodox economic theory which taught that competition was equally necessary to increase the general wealth and strengthen the individual character. These two aims, in the mind of the striver, could not be separated, but if ever his faith was challenged he was more likely to insist on its moral than its worldly advantages. For there were many people then who genuinely thought that they were seeking wealth simply in order to strengthen their character, and so every new success was a tangible proof to them that the strengthening process was going on. A rise in salary was a moral rise; a business promotion, a promotion in spiritual grace. On the other hand, if one mentioned the moral ideal of Socialism to them they would reply that economics had nothing to do with morality, and alternatively or simultaneously that Socialism was immoral, since it did not strengthen the character. The truth is that all economic or political theories, however stripped of moral assumptions, accrete a whole body of moral prejudices and emotions round them in the course of their existence. The *laissez-faire* economists could separate economics and morality with the most satisfactory neatness, but the actual people who by their labour maintained a system based on *laissez-faire* could not achieve that feat, since they were moral beings. So they had either to give *laissez-faire* a high ethical sanction, like the people of whom I have been speaking, or else regard it as evil, like the trade-unionists and Socialists whom I came to know later.

But what raised this religion of getting-on to a really intense faith was the squalor of the surroundings amid which the go-getter lived. The immediate goal that he set before him was not great wealth, but rather respectability, and all his environment reminded him of its opposite. In no place can respectability be a more intense passion than in a town which at every step one takes suggests the very things it fights against: open filth, disorder and degradation. The pushing young Glasgow man felt that he was directly fighting all that this filth, disorder and degradation finally meant: that is, the slums. He could not get away from the slums by ordinary walking on the horizontal plane, for they would always be there when he came back; he could only get away from them by climbing: and in climbing above them he was scoring a symbolical victory over them. In his climb he would have been false to his cause if he had foregone an advantage, even though he knew it injured somebody else; his whole ethic would have been imperilled. That a belief like this was bound to engender insensitiveness is so obvious that I shall make no further apology for saying that it has actually done so.

At the time when I came to Glasgow I could not, of course, know all this, but I read, in the faces of almost every man and youth I met, even in the faces of boys of my own age (I was fourteen), this creed of success which was quite new to me. I had come from a country community where it was a tradition among the small farmers to help one another when help was needed, either with labour or their own goods, and where the only recognized enemy was the landlord, if he happened to be a bad one. In Glasgow, in the particular class I was thrown among first, I found that one's neighbour was one's worst enemy, and one's employer, if not exactly one's best friend, at least the man best worth while keeping in with. In the islands it was considered contemptible to steal a march on your neighbour and tasteless to push yourself forward; but I found that here these things were thought not only permissible but a mark of virtue. I could not reconcile these traits with the kindness and courtesy (outside business) of many of the people who possessed them; and it seems to me still that they are irreconcilable. This division in the nature of these people was due directly to the corrupting influence of Industrialism.

I felt all this very clearly, far more clearly than I could feel it now, but quite blindly. I felt at the same time something else, which was much more terrifying. The best way I can put it is that these people seemed to have all passed through the slums, and to bear the knowledge of the slums within them. On their faces, which were different from the faces I had known before, I thought I could see, quite clearly displayed, a depraved and shameful knowledge, a knowledge which they could not have avoided acquiring, I can see now, but of which they were for the most part unaware. This may sound, to anyone who has lived all his life in an industrial town, exaggerated or wildly improbable; to others it will seem a truism. At any rate I felt this somewhat terrifying warning in people's faces before I had actually seen a slum, for it was several weeks after I came to Glasgow, when I found a post in an office, that I first came in contact with the slums as I walked to and from my work. After that I passed through one of the worst of them twice daily. For it is almost impossible (or was at that time) for anyone working in Glasgow to avoid passing through a slum on his way to and from work, unless he lives in the West End. The people I met did so, for they lived on the south Side, and all the main thoroughfares leading from the town to the South Side were slums or semi-slums.

This depraved knowledge which I found in people's faces was frightening mainly, I think, because the knowledge was concealed from its possessors, and was like a dangerous thing, always with them, whose existence they ignored. Later I came to know Socialists who did not conceal their knowledge of the slums, but talked of it openly, and their faces had not the look I have been trying to describe. When I became a Socialist it was as if in clearly recognizing an outer danger I had killed an inner fear, and it was this, I think, which made the little Socialist gatherings I went to more light-hearted than the ones I had been accustomed to before. But at the time I am speaking of I knew nothing about Socialism, and like everybody else I stubbornly set myself not to see what was before my eyes every day. This in time produced a sense of inward squalor, the reflection of the outward misery that I pushed away from me; and finally I reached a stage where I almost ignored my surroundings, lost the natural delight in my eyes which I had once had, and shielded my senses by shutting them off from what perpetually violated them. I tell this because I feel sure the same thing happens to everybody in an industrial town. All one's surroundings there drive the senses in upon themselves and blind them to one thing after another, until they perform only a utilitarian function. This is bound to happen whether one is conscious of it or not. The great majority of industrial town-dwellers, rich and poor, are unconscious of it; and it is this that makes their response to experience so unlike that both of the artist and of the ordinary peasant, who can still look at things with more than a specialized, classifying eye.

All these things, and doubtless many others which were too subtle for my mind to catch or my memory to re-create, went to produce my first impression of the people I met in Glasgow, making me feel that they were sad and incomprehensible distortions of nature. I describe these impressions because I think that that first criticism of indus-trialism was immediate and clear, and is the typical response of anyone who comes straight to a town like Glasgow from the country. He feels at once that this life is barbarous and degrading, until the unanimous opinion of the people round him that it is perfectly normal works upon him, and he accepts it.

III

The refuse that one finds scattered in the streets of an industrial town has always seemed to me to tell a great deal about it, and to be in a humble way a synopsis of its life. One finds there a miscellaneous and yet representative collection which is very revealing, though it can have little resemblance to the franker contents of medieval or Renaissance streets. Scraps of newspaper, cigarette ends, rims of bowler hats, car tickets, orange peel, boot soles, chocolate paper, fish-and-chip paper, sixpences, broken bottles, pawn tickets, and various human excretions: these several things, clean and dirty, liquid and solid, make up a sort of an industrial town. To this soup must be added an ubiquitous dry synthetic dust, the siftings of the factories, which is capable under rain of turning into a greasy paste resembling mud, but has no other likeness to the natural mire of a country road; for that, however unpleasant underneath one's feet, breathes freshness and has a sweet smell. Sometimes this compost is thickened still more by a brown fog permeated by the same manufactured dirt, with a smell which is neither clean nor obnoxious but is simply the generalized smell of factories. In this soup it is considered a perfectly natural thing for human beings to live.

I have passed through most of the slums of Glasgow, but I have never done so unless when forced by necessity, and I have never attempted to investigate them, and would not do so at any price. I listened once to an argument between an Englishman and a Scotsman, both Socialists, on whether England or Scotland had the worst slums, and observed that each was hurt because the other insisted that his country bore off the palm. That taught me a lesson.

Since I began to write this book everybody whom I have asked for information about Glasgow has at once got on to the subject of the slums and enjoyed himself for an hour or two, without my being able to convince him that that was not what I really wanted. I have been told of slum courts so narrow that the refuse flung into them mounted and mounted in the course of years until it blocked all the house windows up to the second-top storey; and I have been given an idea of the stench rising from this rotting, half liquid mass which I shall not reproduce here. I have been told of choked stair-head lavatories with the filth from them running down the stairs; of huge midnight migrations of rats from one block to another; and of bugs crawling down the windows of tram-cars. All these things, I have been assured, are true, and no doubt they are; but I shall not enter into a competition with the narrators of horrors of this kind, for the appetite of moderately well-off and quite well-off people for these infamous morsels is one which has no connection with the sentiment of pity, but is likely to check rather than induce it, creating disgust in its stead. Disgust is the coldest of human emotions, colder than hatred because more self-centred. If one hates the slums one may do something about them; but if one is filled with disgust of them there is nothing but to turn away.

Moreover, it is difficult to define a slum, and a more important fact is that the majority of the population of Glasgow live in some form of poverty caused by the working of the economic system. The insanitary slums are more picturesque, and more thrillingly horrible things can be related of them; but if one could conceive the total volume of colourless or bug-coloured poverty that exists in Glasgow, as in all other cities of its kind, one would be crushed by the knowledge. We manage to live with some comfort simply because we cannot conceive it. The life of the slums is infamous, but it is freer and more various than the life of the decent poor. A slum is a poor quarter in which the people no longer take the trouble to keep up appearances. Nothing in such places makes any attempt to keep up appearances. The houses have a rotten look, and send out a complicated bouquet of mingled stenches. All that respectable society conceals is openly displayed. Language has a flat and commonplace obscenity; knowledge, however vile, is frankly expressed; passions and hatreds let themselves go. All this happens within a sort of invisible cage, whose bars are as strong as iron. It is a life which through the course of generations has acquired a settled convention; for children grow up in these places and are trained from their earliest years in the way of life which is suitable for them. The deepest hope of the decent poor is to bring up their children in a way that will give them the opportunity of a better life than their parents. What distinguishes the slum-dwellers from the decent poor is that they have quite given up this hope, that they are quite static. They see no prospect for themselves or their descendants but the slums. This is because they are the final product of a system; there is nothing beyond them; and their existence has therefore a logic with which there is no arguing.

Yet this does not mean that these people are a special class outside the bounds of humanity, but merely that they are ordinary men and women in a hopeless position, who have been placed there by the operation of a process over which they have no control. That being so, it would surely be inhuman to grudge them what enjoyment they can get, whether in drink, love, or fighting, and stupid to complain, as the benevolent sometimes do, that the hearts of these people are not at once softened by a smile or a few kind words. A natural impulse is to snatch every child away from such places; but even if that could be done the slums would fill up again; the system under which we live forces people into them with a continuous mechanical pressure, and once they are there they may give up all hope: they will become like their neighbours. The sufferings of an ordinary healthy child brought up in the slums are dreadful beyond imagination. The terror and corrupt knowledge of these children can be heard in their voices, the most desolate and discordant sound in creation. This terror breaks out in early youth, that is as soon as these boys are strong enough to fight for themselves, in revengeful violence and cruelty. This process coincides with puberty, it is automatic, and kind words and boys' clubs will never have more than a passing effect on it.

The openness of all this slum life in Glasgow makes it impossible for the respectable who come in contact with it every day not to build up some attitude to it. The general attitude is simple reprobation, an explicit declaration that all slum-dwellers are incurably depraved and outside the human pale. This attitude makes people ignore the slums as irrelevant to ordinary life, and leads to that suppression of knowledge which I read in so many faces when I first came to Glasgow. The more humane generally hold that a great deal can be done by kindness and goodwill. There are others again, also humane, who take an objective interest in the slum-dwellers as a curious species of humanity with a flavour of their own. I can give an instance of this.

When I was eighteen I stayed in the same lodgings as a young Highlander, six or seven years older than myself. With his Highland courtesy he contrived to give me very good advice and unobtrusively keep his eye on me, showing a most delicate nicety of consideration in everything which concerned us both. I was in the first stages of my conversion to Socialism and he was troubled about my state, for he was a pious conservative. We were arguing one day about Socialism, when he told me a story he had heard which indirectly supported his view that things should be left as they were. It was about a newsboy. For several years he had stood at a certain street corner in Glasgow, barefoot both in summer and winter. A regular customer of his, a kind-hearted man, taking pity on his feet blue with cold, presented him with boots and stockings. The boy thankfully accepted them, but a few days after he began to wear them he went down with pneumonia and died in hospital. Now my friend, who was one of the kindest-hearted men I have ever known, simply regarded this as an interesting example of low life; he was sincerely sorry for the boy, but it never occurred to him that the boy's existence was other than it should be, and the moral of his story was that the *status quo* should not be interfered with. I tell this incident because it illustrates a respectable attitude to the slums, which though infinitely preferable to the ordinary attitude of suppression, is as strictly conditioned.

The most revolting and illuminating attitude to the slums that I ever encountered in Glasgow was held by a kind-hearted theosophist. Theosophists are people who have very little difficulty in believing things, and his belief was that the people in the slums were suffering for sins which they had committed in a former existence, so that any betterment of their lot would nullify this act of expiation and be spiritually wrong. The fact that as slum-dwellers they had no knowledge of those former sins did not matter to him in the least. Now there had been a peculiarly horrible murder committed about that time. A young woman had been found in a wood with various knife wounds on her body and the marks of a man's teeth on her throat; and it seemed to me that if some morning a police constable were to call at my innocent theosophist's house, seize him, pry open his mouth, announce: 'The marks were made by your teeth', haul him off to prison and have him tried and condemned, he would be in exactly the same position as the slum-dwellers he thought of as suffering for former sins of which they could never know. The slum-dwellers are not condemned to death, it is true, but merely to lifelong imprisonment; but that is an infinitely more dreadful punishment. The more I thought of the theosophist's idea, the more I was impressed by its truth as a picture of the life of a slum-dweller. Any theory at all, however ludicrous, which attempts to account for a thing, makes us see it more completely than before. And taking away the comforting theosophical moral, it is as if an invisible police inspector had seized all the inhabitants of the slums at some stage in their lives, in infancy before they could speak, in manhood, in old age, and haled them to a judge to be sentenced for life for a crime of which they were quite unaware. They commit other crimes in plenty, no doubt, but they never committed this one, which they could not understand even if it were explained to them. That is a measure of their hopelessness.

The squalor of the slum-dwellers' lives in Glasgow is one reason for the respectable attitudes which I have tried to describe. A stronger reason is their open publication of their degradation, which springs partly from their hopelessness and partly from a feeling that it is wrong that misery and vice such as theirs should be ignored. This public flaunting of degradation is one of the things which distinguish the Scottish from the English slums. Probably it arises from a last-ditch sentiment of justice. To publish one's degradation is a moral protest. The London slums are dreary; but the Glasgow slums always hold a sense of possible menace; they take their revenge on the respectable and the rich if in nothing else in compelling them to grow a still thicker hide of insensibility and suppression. That revenge may appear small, but its effects are beyond computation. There can be hardly any decent Glaswegian but has seen some sight in passing through the slums which he afterwards wanted to erase from his memory. Such memories should be kept open, not hidden away in places where they fester, for that is the only hope both for those who suppress them and for the eventual health of society. But it is easier to say this than to do it. For the life of an average member of the respectable classes in Glasgow is a direct fight against the slums, and in that fight suppression and insensibility are invaluable weapons, and as long as society continues to be competitive they will be used. Thus the existence of the slums and of poverty in general poisons the life of a community in all sorts of hidden ways. It is this settled almost comfortable poisoned state which I have tried to give some idea of. It is the generic state of Industrialism.

IV

The slums not only penetrate the lives of all classes in Glasgow, affecting their ideas and their most personal emotions, perhaps going with them into their bedrooms, but also send out a dirty wash into the neatest and remotest suburbs and even the surrounding countryside, so that it is possible for one to feel that the whole soil for miles around is polluted. This is partly, no doubt, because the slums of Glasgow are distributed over a very large area and in a very irregular form, so that it is difficult even in the West End to get very far away from them. Some of them are on the outskirts, like Polmadie and Springburn; others occupy a large area of the centre of the town at either end of Argyle Street; the older part of the South Side is honeycombed with them from east to west; and there is another large area from the Cowcaddens to Garscube Road extending for a considerable distance into the north-west, which is the rich and fashionable quarter.

To the south-east between Polmadie and Rutherglen the city

ended when I came to it first in country which could only be called slum country. (That has since been covered, much to its improvement, by new houses.) There, if one wanted to get country air, one had to walk past several squalid rows of miners' hovels among which a farmhouse had been forlornly stranded, with a piggery of surpassing stench. After that came a country road called the Hundred Acre Dyke, dotted with a few ringwormed trees, and affording a bleak prospect of smoking pits and blackened fields. This was a great resort of lovers on Sunday evenings. If one turned to the right until one passed the little town of Cathcart, now a part of Glasgow, one reached a pleasant enough country road. But the first stretch was, like the immediate surroundings of almost all industrial towns, a debased landscape in which every growing thing seemed to be poisoned and stunted, a landscape which involuntarily roused evil thoughts and seemed made to be the scene of murders and rapes.

There was another stretch of country to the northwest beyond Anniesland, which, although it was without coal-pits or factories, had for some reason the same character. There was a meanly wicked-looking wood there where lovers wandered in the evenings, and this wood was periodically infested by hooligans who spied on these young couples and sometimes tried to blackmail them. The country between Polmadie and Rutherglen was one of the most desolate of these tracts. There were several small coal-pits there, and walking on a Sunday afternoon through the black slag paths one would see stunted naked boys bathing in the filthy pools, from which rose a smell of various acids and urine. Respectable people also took their constitutional there and stared at the tattered trees which rose from that scabbed landscape. If one walked out for a few miles one could get away from this scene and into real country. But such places seemed to have an attraction, and the crowds there were far thicker than they were a few miles out.

The slums in a Scottish industrial town are generally to be found either near the factories or in the oldest and most dilapidated of the tenements. Glasgow has slums of both kinds. There are certain factories which produce such a stench that to live near them involves a loss of self-respect, and the surrounding houses in such cases turn into slums. Many such factories are scattered over the South Side. On the other hand the tenements near the shipyards have mostly a clean and orderly look; and one can still feel (though they have degenerated a great deal since ship-building virtually stopped) that the people who lived in them led for many years a self-respecting existence and had a tradition. And immediately behind some of the shipyards one may come upon green fields dotted with trees. Shipbuilding does not pollute the air or ravage the soil as coal-mining does, and the comparative cleanliness of his work gives the shipyard worker, I think, a peculiar self-respect, or did at one time, when there was something for him to do.

This extraordinarily wide distribution of the slum areas in Glasgow may actually be good in some ways for the spiritual health of its people. The strength of the Socialist Party in Glasgow is probably due in part to this impossibility of getting away from the slums.

In Henry Grey Graham's *Social Life in Scotland in the Eighteenth Century*, one of the best books ever written on Scotland, there is a very attractive description of Glasgow as it was about 1730. Graham was a man who did not sentimentalize the past; indeed his picture of life in eighteenth-century Scotland is a very dark one. He quotes the testimony of Edward Burt, an 'English engineer officer', who visited the city in 1726. 'It has,' said Burt,

'a spacious carrefour where stands the cross, and going round it you have by turns the views of the four streets that in regular angles proceed from thence. The houses are faced with ashlar stone; they are well sashed, all of one model, and piazzas rise round them on either side, which gives a good air to the buildings. There are some handsome streets; but the extreme parts of the town are mean and disagreeable to the eye.'

He thought the town 'the most uniform and prettiest' that he had ever seen. Another witness quoted by Graham – McUre, the first historian of Glasgow – describes the town as

'surrounded with cornfields, kitchen and flower gardens, and beautiful orchards, abounding with fruits of all sorts, which, by reason of the open and large streets, send forth a pleasant, odoriferous smell.'

Graham adds, with his usual common-sense realism:

'Beside the substantial houses of the well-to-do citizens, with quaint picturesque Flemish architecture and crow-stepped gables, however, stood mean, dirty, and broken-down hovels to mar the beauty of the town; while in the streets stood middens, against which magistrates vainly objected, and in the gutters remained garbage seriously to spoil the 'odoriferous smell' of the fruit- and flower-scented air.'

It was the Union with England that first started Glasgow on its road to prosperity. Before that Scotland had not been allowed to trade with Virginia (which was a strict English preserve). Through the trade in tobacco Glasgow increased greatly both in wealth and population. The tobacco trade collapsed in 1776 with the outbreak of the American war, plunging many of the tobacco lords into bankruptcy. But in 1754 James Watt had come to Glasgow from Greenock, and it was while he was walking in the Glasgow Green one Sunday afternoon that 'the idea of the steam condenser flashed upon his mind'. That Sunday walk, along with the presence of coal and iron within easy reach and the Clyde at its gate, did more than anything else to decide the subsequent fate of the town and make possible its enormous wealth and its enormous squalor. In the nineteenth century the town increased by leaps and bounds and quite haphazardly, and it is still increasing, though prosperity has left it. Before 1707 the town's population was a little over 12,500; by 1800 it was almost 80,000; now it is over a million. This rapid and enormous increase was due mainly to the neighbouring iron and coal mines, and to shipping and shipbuilding. Scottish iron is almost at a standstill; coal is declining; and shipping and shipbuilding in Britain generally have sunk so definitely that not even optimists expect them to be again what they once were, except in the event of another war. The probable consequence seems to be that Glasgow, after its rapid expansion, is fated to shrink again. A competitive system can provide for expansion; indeed expansion is a necessary condition for its smooth working. But it can make no provision at all for contraction; and if Glasgow is to decrease in size, which seems unavoidable, if Scotland, after its feverish burst of industrialism, is to relapse into a predominantly agricultural state again, which seems possible, something besides the mere operation of the competitive system will be needed to effect that transition. It is a feeling of the imminence of this problem which, among other things, has led to the spread of Nationalism. But Nationalism without a social programme, and a radical one, will be quite impotent to deal with it.

If all this were actually to happen, if industrial Scotland, having exhausted itself, were to disappear, leaving the black coal and iron country to be reclaimed by the peasant, it might seem that the immense effort of growth which we call Industrialism had been wasted: a mere brute fact of history, a devastation without meaning. But one has only to turn to Graham's picture of life in eighteenth-century Scotland to see that that is not so, and to recognize the necessity of the industrial phase. In his chapter on 'The Land and the People' he tells of the famine years which began the eighteenth century.

'From one end of the country to the other the poorer classes of the population of above a million were in misery, hunger, and in the shadow of death . . . The sheep and oxen died in thousands, the prices of everything among a peasantry that had nothing went up to famine pitch, and a large proportion of the population in rural districts was destroyed by disease and want. During these 'hungry years', as starvation stared the people in the face, the instincts of self-preservation overpowered all other feelings, and even natural affection became extinct in crowds of men and women forced to prowl and fight for their food like beasts. People in the north sold their children to slavery in the plantations for victuals: men struggled with their sisters for a morsel of bread; many were so weak and dispirited that they had neither heart nor strength to bury their dead. On the roads were to be seen dead bodies with a morsel of raw flesh in their mouths, and dying mothers lying with starved infants which had sucked dry breasts; while numbers, dreading lest their bodies should be exposed to the birds, crawled, when they felt the approach of death, to the kirkyard, that they might have some better chance of being buried when death overtook them . . . Even in the streets of towns starving men fell down and died.'

And he quotes a contemporary witness, Patrick Walker, the old Covenanter.

'Through the long continuation of these manifold judgements,' says Walker, 'deaths and burials were so common that the living wearied of burying the dead. I have seen corpses drawn on sleds, many neither having coffins or winding-sheets. I was one of four who carried the corpse of a young woman a mile of way, and when we came to the grave an honest man came and said, 'You must go and help me to bury my son; he is lien dead these two days; otherwise I will be obliged to bury him in my own yard.' We went, and there were eight of us had two miles to carry the corpse of this young man, many neighbours looking on, but none to help. I was credibly informed that in the north two sisters on a Monday's morning were found carrying the corpse of their brother with bearing ropes, none offering to help. I have seen some walking about till the sun-setting, and to-morrow about six o'clock in the summer's morning found dead, their heads lying in their hands, and mice and rats having eaten a great part of their hands and arms.'

This is what happened in years of famine, when the crops failed; but years of famine seem to have been pretty frequent. In good years the ordinary people lived in poverty far surpassing that of a modern slum. Graham says:

'In 1702 Morer, the English chaplain, described the houses of the vulgar as "low and feeble, their walls made of a few stones jumbled together without mortar to cement 'em, so ordered that it does not cost much more time to erect such a cottage than to pull it down," without chimneys, and only holes in the turf-covered roofs for smoke to pass. His description will apply to the houses of the people through a great part of the eighteenth century. The hovels of one room were built of stones and turf, without mortar, the holes in the wall stuffed with straw, or heather, or moss, to keep out the blasts. The fire, usually in the middle of the house floor, in despair of finding an exit by the smoke-clothed roof, filled the room with malodorous clouds. The cattle at night were tethered at one end of the room, while the family lay at the other on heather on the floor. The light came from an opening at either gable, which, whenever the wind blew in, was stuffed with brackens or an old bonnet to keep out the sleet and blast. The roofs were so low in northern districts that the inmates could not stand upright, but sat on the stones or three-legged stools that served for chairs, and the huts were entered by doors so low and narrow that to gain an entrance one required almost to creep. Their thatching was of ferns and heather, for the straw was all needed for the cattle. Yet, foul, drab, and fetid as they were, the people liked these hovels for their warmth.'

This dirt and poverty gave rise to a great deal of disease; and the people, being religious, accepted the epidemics that swept large numbers of them away as visitations from God. Women grew old and lost their looks very early. And the whole country got a bad name for the skin disease that infested it.

Graham ascribes a great part of this poverty to ignorance and superstition.

'Piety did not uproot this inveterate sluggishness of farmer and labourer; it seemed rather to dignify dirt and consecrate laziness. The people believed that disease was due to the hand of God, instead of being due to the want of using their own hands. They held that every season of dearth was owing to Providence rather than to their own improvidence. They protested that weeds were a consequence of Adam's fall, and that to remove docks, wild mustard, and nettles was to undo the divine curse. They threshed the corn with the flail, and winnowed it by throwing it up in the air, rather than use the outlandish fanners which Meikle had set up in 1770; because "it was making Devil's wind," contravened Scripture, which said, "The wind bloweth where it listeth," and took the "power out o' the hands o' the Almighty."'

To read of such past poverty and wretchedness shows what an immense advance has been made since by the increase of things like knowledge and education (which there is a disposition to depreciate at present) and by Industrialism itself, in spite of its evils; and it also gives a reasonable hope that the improvement will continue, a hope all the more justified because we are now in a position to see more clearly perhaps in what direction it lies. The unemployed engineer on the Clyde to-day is better off than the employed peasant in the early eighteenth century; and that is due partly to Industrialism, which has made a higher standard possible, and partly to the growth during the last two centuries of what is called the social conscience, which insists that a higher standard should actually be maintained. Left to itself the Industrial System would clearly have produced during the last decade misery on a scale that would have left Graham's picture far behind. Yet there is no doubt that the evolution of Industrialism itself, by increasing wealth generally, has helped to change our attitude to the poor and make the thought unpleasant that they should die of starvation. In a country where poverty is the norm, as it was in Scotland in the beginning of the eighteenth century, people cannot be expected to pay very scrupulous attention to the degrees of poverty, especially if destitution should be ordained and sometimes directly produced by the hand of God. Starvation in a state of potential plenty is a very different thing: a community which permitted it now would be guilty of a criminal coldness of heart. Scotland in the early eighteenth century was guilty merely of ignorance, superstition and misfortune. There was probably a narrower gulf between the rich man and the starving man then than there is to-day between the wealthy magnate and the unemployed engineer drawing his 15/3.* So it seems that the social conscience, undeniable as its virtues are, operates only within narrow limits, and is content if it can be assured that people are not actually dying of starvation.

The obvious truth is that the problem at the present stage is not starvation at all. It cannot be in a world where wheat is burned and herring thrown back into the sea. Every age has its own problems, and can deal only with them. Scotland got over its starving eighteenth-century phase by applying reason to its agriculture in the first place, and by the rise of the Industrial System in the second. The problem of our time is how to make the Industrial System work to everybody's benefit. 15/3 a week can certainly keep a single man alive; it cannot possibly provide him with a life that is desirable. The unemployed married man is still worse off, and his children, if they get only what the Government allows them, are worst off of all. 8/- is supposed to keep an unemployed man's wife, and 2/- each believed to provide for his children, no matter what their ages may be.

. . . It was a very hot bright day when I went down to see the shipyards that once in my life I had passed every morning. The weather had been good for several weeks, and all the men I saw were tanned and brown as if they had just come back from their summer holidays. They were standing in the usual groups, or walking by twos and threes, slowly, for one felt as one looked at them that the world had

* 15 shillings 3 pence = 76p.

166

not a single message to send them on, and that for them to hasten their steps would have meant a sort of madness. Perhaps at some time the mirage of work glimmered at the extreme horizon of their minds; but one could see by looking at them that they were no longer deceived by such false pictures.

I was on my way to a shipbuilding office where I had once worked for several years. During my time there had been twelve clerks in it; they had now shrunk to six, and the six were on half-time and half-pay. Like the unemployed they were all sunburnt, since they spent half of their days in enforced leisure. The office had always been a pleasant one to work in; for the cashier, an old gentleman now dead, had for fifty years or so resisted the importunities of travellers for newfangled devices such as adding-machines and filing systems, and had stuck to the methods he had found in operation when he entered the office as a junior clerk. When that could have been I have no idea, probably about 1860. We were all proud of him, and grateful for the way in which he left us to ourselves: I have never been in a little community where such an idyllic and quietistic atmosphere reigned. Something of it still remained when I paid my visit. So my old friends, instead of being embittered by the bad turn of shipbuilding, were philosophic and resigned. Nevertheless, it was sad to revisit the place and remember the time when it had been filled with hope: a hope which in it, as in a hundred other workshops and offices in the Clyde, is now hardly more than a memory. Thousands of young men started out a little over twenty years ago with the ambition of making a modest position in the world, of marrying a wife and founding a family. And thousands of them have seen that hope vanish, probably never to return for the rest of their lives. This is surely one of the most astonishing signs of our time: the disappearance in whole areas of society of a hope so general at one time that not to have it would have seemed unnatural. As for the generation of unemployed who have arisen since the war, many of them are not even acquainted with this hope . . .

V

Here I think I had better go back and give some impressions of these people, now unemployed, as I knew them years ago when they were working and Industrialism on the Clyde still seemed to have a long and vigorous life before it. I have already said all that I want to say about the business mystics whom I chanced to meet first of all; I suppose they might be described as middle-class people striving to become upper middle-class. All of them really belonged to the working class, but because their eyes were fixed on a brighter goal and they wore smartly cut suits and bowler hats instead of dungarees and caps, this fact was magically concealed from them, and if taxed with it they indignantly denied it.

Being a poorly paid clerk, I also belonged to this class, and I only came in contact with that part of the working class which acknowledges that it is working class when I joined in turn a Socialist club called the Clarion Scouts, the ILP, and my union, the National Union of Clerks.

If I were to try to define the difference between the class I left and the class I entered then, I should find it very difficult: but I think it would be true to say that the genuine workman had far more freedom of mind, more generosity of feeling, and a considerably more delicate sense of honour than the sham one. To unite with one's fellow-workers for a common aim, in a union or some other body, is no doubt an aim which is finally based on interest; but it is also one which demands a certain disinterestedness from the units composing it. A trade union seeks to advance the good of all its members, Socialism to secure the good of everybody, and such an ideal is by any standards higher than the ideal of mere individual self-advancement which was held by the class I had known first. That class, or such members of it as thought about the matter at all, held that in doing the best for himself a man was serving the highest interests of society; and they never saw that this was a belief so fatally convenient that it allowed a man to follow his bent as much as he pleased, while imposing upon him no obligations whatever except the obligation of keeping the law, and if he was a religious man of observing such religious commands as squared with his economic interest. His obligations, in other words, were vague and general. They were matters of belief: he believed, for instance, that God existed, that Christ died for him (if he was an evangelical Christian), that theft, murder, adultery, and various other things, such as drinking and swearing, were bad, and that the British Empire was the greatest of all institutions. He might believe also, if he liked, that Roman Catholicism was the Scarlet Woman, that mixed bathing was an abomination and Sabbath-breaking blasphemous; but as he had no urgent temptation to indulge in any of these sins except, perhaps, adultery, the avoidance of them imposed no real sacrifice on him: they were pictured and framed sins which he hung up in his life because they were an expected part of its furniture. He professed a Christianity which had no connection even with the means by which he contrived the feat of living, that is his daily business; a concern for the good of society which permitted him to do the same things that an inveterate enemy of it might have done with equal reason; and a patriotism, for the Empire or for Scotland or for both, which was merely a pleasant and warmth-giving emotion. In other words, he professed a great number of moral sentiments, but the most important part of his life, the part he spent at work, was quite uninfluenced by moral considerations, being ruled merely by considerations of legality. As most of the men I am speaking of were professing Christians, one cannot help thinking that the Scottish Church, by its weak or politic or merely worldly policy of trimming, has been largely responsible for this false state of things. There are many among the younger Scottish ministers now of whom nobody could say this; but the damage was done before their time, and I doubt whether they will be able to undo it.

Now among the trade union workers whom I met there did not exist this accepted and complacent division between profession and practice; and their relation to one another was not merely a self-seeking relation cloaked in moral sentiments, but a real moral relation. Their obligations to one another were obligations for which if necessary they had to make sacrifices. They were pledged neither to take any advantage of their neighbours, nor to rise in the world at their expense. These are moral principles, and, socially speaking, among the most fundamental of moral principles. The remarkable thing is that these trade-unionists not only held them, but also practised them. The business mystics might have gone to these workmen to learn what morality is; since there can be no morality without practical obligations.

One of my first surprises then, after I joined the ILP and came in contact with the trade unions, was the discovery that moral theories were not necessarily mere words, but could be taken quite seriously and a real attempt be made to put them into practice. The men who tried to practise them were not solemn or pious about them; they hardly ever spoke of them, and took them mostly for granted. But they had a tradition to keep up, and a tradition produces a delicate sense of honour; and they were pledged not to overreach one another, and that is the basis of disinterested communication between human things. I had been amazed at some of the friendships I had known among my old acquaintances; friendships in which natural affection and calculation were inextricably interwoven, and which were largely held together by the reciprocal giving away of good business tips in the expectation that better ones would be received in return. These men constantly talked of their own business: the workmen talked of their union or of this or that change which affected industry or society, and their conversation was consequently far more interesting, for nothing could be more wearisome than dialogues consisting of: 'Do you know how many orders I got to-day?' or: 'Fancy how much our firm paid out in wages last Saturday!' which I have overheard a thousand times in the third-class carriage of Glasgow suburban trains, carried on by animated young men.

I am speaking of the trade unions twenty-odd years ago, not as they must be now that the semi-stoppage of industry and the pressure of capitalists have weakened them. If there had existed a statesman of sufficient disinterestedness at that time, he could have made these men and their unions the basis of a new society, for nowhere else would he have found such incorruptibility, or such a sincere desire to secure the general good. They had virtues on which such a man could have absolutely depended; they were strongly organized; and they had a discipline which they had themselves created. If a single policy unambiguously embodying the good of society had been put before them, they would have responded to it, and they would have had sufficient strength, with such a lead, to carry it through. A great number of these men are now living in semi-starvation on the dole; their sons, who might have carried on the tradition which they created, do not know what work or responsibility or discipline is; their unions barely contrive to remain in existence. If Capitalism manages finally to smash these unions, it will be a loss to civilization greater than the loss that would be brought about by another war.

There were many among these men who spent all their hard-won evenings in working for their unions or for Socialism. They did this without expecting or receiving any reward. They started classes, spoke at meetings or sold 'literature', as it was called; kept their members together; and attended to the business side of their branches. Some of them believed that Socialism would come in their time; the majority that it would not come until after their death. The practical historical result of their work was the Labour Party, and the elevation of Mr J. H. Thomas and Mr J. Ramsay Macdonald. In integrity of character and grasp of the real problems of the time often far above their leaders, they went on doing the tasks which they saw had to be done, and refusing the temptations which were offered them. They saw before them the life of a workman; that is, a life which could never escape into riches or even into moderate comfort. They embraced that life without a thought of rising from it except along with all their fellow-workmen. If such devotion and fidelity are not to be admired, then all our ideas of morality are mistaken.

There were others who studied philosophy and literature, and tried to understand the past. Among them were men of first-class intelligence, who, given a better opportunity, would have been heard of in the world. I have met among them Hegelians, Schopenhauerians, Spencerians, and even Nietzscheans; and the one thing one could generally depend upon in them was that they knew their subject and had served a regular apprenticeship to it, just as they did to the trades they followed. Occasionally one came across scatter-brained readers among them, who hopelessly jumbled up all the knowledge they had acquired and used it merely for display. But these were a small minority: the discipline of learning a trade and the exactitude required to practise it were in their bones, and when they took up a subject they set themselves to master it as if it were a handicraft. More of them turned to philosophy and science than to literature; I think naturally. I am trying to give some impression of the actual human beings who are hidden behind statistics of unemploy-ment; I do not claim that the men I have been speaking of form a majority of them; but I have no doubt whatever that they are among them. What reparation can be offered to these men by society, for which they have worked unselfishly, and without considering their own advantage?

VII

[Muir describes (VI) the rich of Glasgow but he goes on to point out an underlying resemblance between the rich and the poor of the city: neither sets much value on rank and privilege.]

A sadder distinguishing characteristic of the Glasgow man (and it cuts across all classes) is the mark that has been visibly impressed upon him by Industrialism, in the lineaments of his face and the shape and stature of his body. If one were set down in the middle of Glasgow without knowing what town one was in and without seeing a single factory or slum, one would know by looking at the people passing that one was in an industrial city. Certainly one would see many remarkable and eloquent faces, from which one could read more perhaps than from the polite masks of Edinburgh; but a great number of them would show that characteristic distortion which one finds in industrial regions, and there alone. The mixture of races in Glasgow might have been fortunate enough in itself, being partly Lowland, partly Highland, and partly Irish; drawn, that is to say, from regions which produce men of good and sometimes beautiful physique. Thrown together in Glasgow amid completely different conditions, these men and women have suffered a violent transformation, and the characteristic products of their marriage to the Industrial System, their residence in the crucible, are squat and lumpy but very powerful physical types, and small, neat and agile ones. These types are perhaps the most fit to survive in an industrial civilization; authorities on race, who are, however, probably the most undependable of all authorities, have asserted it. At any rate, such types can be found in great numbers in all classes in Glasgow, and give a special character to Glasgow crowds. Yet in spite of the change which they have suffered in their very physical frame, or perhaps partly because of it, there are more interesting faces to be found in Glasgow crowds than anywhere else, probably, in Scotland. The faces I am particularly thinking of give the impression of having passed through a prolonged test resembling some mysterious illness, from which they have emerged with their humanity and goodness intact. One sees such faces sometimes among the physically de-formed; it is very strange and moving to see them among men and women physically vigorous. Sitting in Glasgow theatres, I have often been astonished by a sudden glimpse of some man's or woman's face with this particular look, which was like an unconscious revelation.

VIII

I have lingered for a long time in Glasgow, and yet I feel that I have given a very inadequate idea of its actual being as a community. Glasgow contains such a number of things: thousands of families living in harmony or in dissension, comfortably or poorly, in anything from one small room to twenty large ones: slums, villas and turreted mansions, varying in comfort, but alike in ugliness: factories, at work or silent: socialist societies and YMCAs: churches, Catholic chapels and Orange halls: cinemas, dance-halls, tea-rooms and hotel lounges: literary societies: brothels: graveyards: trains and tram-cars where a whole population seems to be in migration: Labour Ex-changes with queues waiting before the doors: streets of prostitutes:

young men waiting for young women at a thousand corners: football-matches: gymnasiums: Salvation Army bands: fathers and mothers beating their children in cold suburban parlours: bands of misguided or desperate youths, who call themselves 'The Norman Conks', or by some other name, roaming about the slums: professors: drinking clubs: street fights: black-coated congregations dispersing from a thousand churches, Catholic, Protestant, Baptist, Wesleyan, Unitarian: unemployed men walking about in a vacuum represented by one or two or five or ten years: boxing-matches and theosophical lectures: luxurious shops and shebeens: curtains discreetly raised and lowered in suburban streets: bun-fights: Band of Hope concerts: bridge drives: law-courts: schools: prisons: official receptions: and a thousand things more which paralyse the mind when it tries to number them. A modern city is strictly inconceivable. Consequently I have kept very largely to the economic side of Glasgow life, because it is the essential one: the other aspects of modern towns have become journalism. I actually intended at one point to say something about the churches, and in particular about the furious clashes between Orangemen and Catholics which fill the cells of the lock-ups after every St Patrick's Day. But these things do not matter; they have only a fictitious importance; and to try to understand an Orangeman's state of mind in any case would not only be extraordinarily difficult, but also quite profitless, for the Orange superstition is surely one of the most insensate of existing superstitions, and also one of the most uninteresting. Unfortunately the Orange demonstrators and marchers belong mainly to the working class, just as the Catholic ones do. This feud causes a great deal of trouble, and has not even the excuse of being justified by interest. It is sheer inane loss: a form of hooliganism under the cover of something too silly even to be called an idea. But in the final count it comes to almost nothing. The fundamental realities of Glasgow are economic. How is this collapsing city to be put on its feet again?

The Highlands

[Muir's tour of the Highlands took him, in the 1921 Standard car given to him by a friend, from Perth to Inverness and then to Ullapool on the West Coast where he arrived one day at lunch-time. His hotel was full of English people, who had imposed a code of etiquette, including pre-dinner cocktails, on their fellow guests.]

In the afternoon I went for a stroll through the soft rain. The streets lay empty in their wet whiteness. On the dripping pier a young Highlander with a waterproof apron tied round his kilt was waiting beside a motor-boat. The waters of the loch were quite smooth. I walked up and down the pier for some time until I found a run of wooden steps leading down to an underground gallery almost level with the sea. There, protected from the rain, I walked about for a long time, listening to the drip of the water from the planks overhead and the murmur of the tide as it sluggishly flowed round the rotting piles. Innumerable star-fish, living and dead, were glued to the glistening black baulks, and shoals of little fishes skimmed over them every now and then as heedlessly as if they belonged to a different world. The water dripped, filling the little gallery with tiny echoes that sounded like shivering glass. I do not know why, but soft rain in the Highlands makes them seem twice as remote, so that one cannot imagine they are within reach of anywhere. A boy and a young woman presently appeared with a collection of suitcases and got into the motor-boat along with the young Highlander. The engine started and in a few minutes they had all been swallowed up in the mist.

I went to bed early to escape a threatened hand at bridge. When I tried to start the car next morning I could make nothing of it. A young mechanic belonging to the hotel tinkered gravely with the plugs for a while. The garage attendants in the Lowlands had always shown a sympathetic, humorous interest in my conveyance; but this young

Highlander treated it with as much respectful concern as if it had been a Rolls-Royce, and did not give the faintest sign that he saw its comic possibilities. He was not really any kinder than the Lowland mechanics had been, but he showed a different consideration for my feelings, or rather for what I might conceivably have felt; for the garage happened to be filled with a dozen cars, all of which looked splendid beside mine, and it would have been easy for any hard-pressed garage hand to regard my engine troubles with impatience. But nothing of the kind happened, and I felt again that I was in a different country.

Up to Ullapool I had been driving over good and moderately level roads. From now on I was to find myself climbing up and down mountain sides over surfaces little better than a cart-track. There must have been something wrong with the plugs, as the young mechanic had said; at any rate I noticed that on the first gradient the car seemed to be complaining more than usual. Then I came to a long, rough, steep rise. I got up full speed and covered a little stretch of it in third gear, then switched to second, and finally to first. The car went more and more slowly, seemed to waver for a moment, and stopped. I was only two-thirds up the hill, hanging precariously at what seemed to me an angle of forty-five degrees. I started the engine again, speeded it up until it roared, slipped the clutch into first gear, jerked the car up a few yards, and then rested it. In this way, by a series of jerks, I got the car up to the top, hoping that this was the worst hill I would have to climb. About a dozen powerful easy-moving cars from the hotel passed me while I was in the middle of this grass-hopper act. My hopes that I had survived the worst, however, were soon dashed; for I presently found myself jerking up a still worse mountain. If I had known more about the car I might have saved myself a great deal of distress for the next few days, for I am certain that there must have been something wrong with the plugs. As it was I was doomed to jerk myself up all the hill roads of the western and northern Highlands from Ullapool to Tongue, and sweat and curse among the strangest and most magnificent scenery. At one point in this curious journey I jerked off without knowing it a suitcase containing all my clothes; the engine was making too much noise for anything else to be heard. But I shall come to that later; and this is all I intend to say about my troubles with the car. They filled my mind in the most curious way, nevertheless, creating a sort of little private hell from which I looked out like Dives on to the heavenly beauty of the north-western Highland mountains.

The thing which impresses one most about the wild scenery in this part of the Highlands is its strangeness. Geologists give the explanation that the mountains here consist of two formations which have piled up in confusion, so that the summits belonging to one of them sometimes burst through the surface of the other. One's actual impression of these peaks is that they do not belong to the world we know at all, but to a much older one; I had this feeling before I knew the geological explanation of it. The ordinary sensations which mountains arouse do not fit these extraordinary rock shapes; and yet they are not terrifying in any way, but merely strange beyond the power of the mind to fathom. Part of their strangeness may, no doubt, be explained by the abruptness with which they start up out of places which seem to have no connection with them. The movement of wild mountain scenery is generally a tossing movement as of waves. On the surface the scenery of Western Sutherlandshire has this tossing movement, but the summits of which I have been speaking rise out of these billows like rocks out of a sea and seem to have a different consistency and to belong to a different order. They are bold and regular and yet unexpected in their shape, as if they were the result of a wild kind of geometry. One sees huge cones with their tops smoothly sliced off to form a circular plateau, gigantic pyramids, and even shapes that seem top-heavy, so that one cannot understand on what principle they remain upright. Round about these isolated peaks rolls in large even swells a sea of lower mountains, from whose shapes one can perceive that they have been moulded by time, for they have its rise and fall and its continuity of rhythm. But these older cones and pyramids seem to have no connection with time at all; they are unearthly not in any vague but in a quite solid sense, like blocks of an unknown world scattered blindly over a familiar one. The thoughts they evoke are neither heavenly nor terrifying, but have a sort of objective strangeness and give one the same feeling one might have if one could have a glimpse of an eternal world, such as the world of mathematics, which had no relation to our human feelings, but was composed of certain shapes which existed in complete changeless autonomy.

Having jerked myself up several hills I landed at last at Kylesku Ferry, where I found I had to wait three hours for the tide. By this time the sun had come out again and the sea in the little inland loch was bright blue against the purplish-grey mountains. I found that I had done six miles an hour and that my right arm was sore with changing gears and pulling the brake. When I arrived I found a family of Australians, a father and two daughters, who had been at the hotel in Ullapool, and they told me that they too had been quite overawed by the cocktail ceremony, so that they had not dared to open their mouths. They told me also that they found it much easier to talk to people in Scotland than in England. They had begun their holiday in London, but during the fortnight they had stayed in a hotel there they had not spoken to a single human being except for the hotel servants. We talked of this and of the Highland deer forests, one of which took up all the hills and valleys we were looking at. With the incoming tide jelly-fishes in great numbers began to float past the little point where we sat. Except for two or three huts beside the ferry there was not a human habitation in sight. Nor in all the expanse of tree-less deer forest could I see a single movement to betray the presence of a living creature.

North from Kylesku I escaped the steep hills for a time, and the landscape in general became lower and more ordinary. As I reached the sea the car wound in and out among rocky gorges for a time. Then I suddenly found myself looking down on a bay filled with small rocky islets, and far beyond them, on the horizon, the long misty outline of Lewis. I stopped for a while to enjoy the unexpected-ness of the sight, for these little islets had the strangeness which I had felt in the high geometrical peaks, and seemed to belong to the same world, reproducing it on a small scale. Whether I was right in thinking this, I do not know; it is difficult to tell which world one is in as one passes through these landscapes, especially if, like myself, one has little or no knowledge of geology. Or that little drove of islands – they seemed to be nothing but rock, and yet an odd tree or two grew from them – may have belonged to a private world of their own. All I know is that they seemed as remote from human life as the huge peaks, and as impervious to all the sentimental associations which nature usually evokes in one's mind. There were one or two cottages on the shore overlooking this tiny archipelago, and smoke was rising from their chimneys in the calm evening air, a sight which for a reason I know of always awakens in me a host of sentimental memories; but here it awakened none at all; the impression of strangeness given by the little islands was too strong.

One could imagine oneself being so deeply influenced by this scenery, if one lived close to it for a long time, that one's most simple feelings about human life would be changed. I think something of this kind must have happened in the little town of Scourie, to which I presently came. In its very formation it seems to be in two minds, like the landscape around it. The houses that make it up are planted at the most abrupt intervals; one finds two or three quite close together, then a few fields, another house, fields again, a hotel on a little rise, a row of houses beyond it that have the air of belonging to a suburban avenue, a farm to one side, and at a good distance from all these, as if it existed in itself, a pier and harbour at the head of a neat and narrow little firth. Not very far from the pier, but away from the village, is a beautiful old house such as one would expect to find in the more cultivated parts of the Borders, and immediately behind it rises a wild hill of bare rippling rock. Beyond the hotel, at a little distance, rises another hill of the same rippling black rock, at whose foot lies a loch, black as ink, and by its look very deep. The village shop adjoins the hotel, and a group of well-set-up young men were standing talking and laughing in front of it when I arrived. It was Saturday evening.

The hotel was comfortably filled with English anglers, a peaceful set of men whose dreamy voices filled the dining-room with dim and watery reminiscences, in which one could hear the lapping of lake water and the day-long purling of streams. They drank a great deal of beer in a quiet hypnotic way, and their voices never rose and never stopped, but babbled on in the most tranquil way imaginable, so that one soon began to feel sleepy. I went for a walk along a cart-track leading up one of the hills, from which I could look down into the black loch. The ripples running under the surface of the hill looked exactly like those that break the smoothness of a big wave. The light was quite clear, though it was ten o'clock, and I had definitely for the first time the feeling of being in the real north. I turned back again, for the blackness of the loch was a little frightening, wandered past one or two houses, crossed a foot-bridge over a little stream lined with tall irises, passed through a green field, and found myself at the pier, where a young man and a young woman were washing nets. The youths who had been standing outside the shop were dispersing in groups along the roads, and I returned to the hotel and to my bed.

I started next morning quite early, for I had made up my mind to be at Scrabster next day in time to catch the boat to Orkney; and though the distance was not great, I knew the limitations of the car and did not know what mountains might still lie in front of me. For most of the forenoon I found to my surprise that the going was not very difficult; cool, misty weather had set in, and the engine did not get so hot as usual; the road, having mounted steadily for a while, wound in and out among little broken hills among which were scattered a confusion of small lochs, all black and somewhat sinister-looking; there was no sign of a dwelling, nor of life of any kind, during all this stretch. Presently the sun came out again, showing that I was at the top of an immense long glen sweeping down towards what looked like level land. Five or six crofters' dwellings with no sign of movement about them (for it was Sunday) lay scattered on the vast slopes: and far away in front I thought I could see a faint quivering in the air, which must have been the sea. I passed a house beside the road with its doors and windows shut, and a little distance from it a few cattle in a field, the first of these animals that I have seen since leaving Dunkeld. I let the car roll of itself down the long descent, giving it a needed rest, and at the foot, in a desolation of sand-dunes, perceived a large, white and polished hotel a little distance away from the road. It seemed to have no right to be there; but I surmised the close neighbourhood of a trout loch, and held on for Durness, knowing that it could not be far away. Presently I saw it huddled grey under a great cloud that had come up, a little rickle of houses, half of them uninhabited, half in ruins, all clean as if they had been sand-polished. I went into a tea-room and lunched on cold ham and lemonade.

As I left Durness I saw a round hill rising out of the sea far away to the north-east, whose shape seemed somehow familiar to me. It was, I realized, the hill of Hoy in Orkney, which I had never seen before from this angle; and it seemed strange to me that for the people of Durness that mound must be a constant shape on the horizon, as well known to them as the inside of their houses; and I thought that all our lives are bounded by a similar horizon, which is at once familiar to us and beyond our knowledge, and that it is against this indistinct barrier that our imaginings pile themselves up, building for all of us a fabulous world. I tried to think of Hoy as an outline on the horizon which never came nearer; and because I knew the Orkneys, having lived in them during my childhood, I had a sense stronger than ever before of the double aspect of everything, and realized that if it had been possible for me to live in two places at once, in Durness, say, and my father's farm in Orkney, my life there would have seemed to one part of me merely a dream in the shadow of that round hill rising from the sea. This thought disturbed me, for it seemed to point to a sort of ultimate isolation of every human being, an isolation produced by the mere workings of time and space, which therefore no ideal state or Utopia could ever reform away. I told myself that this was a figment of my imagination, but knew it was not as I looked at that hill which I seemed to know by two faculties at once, which I had so much wished to see, but had never expected to see like this. And I reflected that all the strange scenery which I had gazed at during my two-days' journey had just as little relation to it as it was known by the few people who lived among it, as that round hill in the sea to Orkney.

Somewhat east of Durness the long and narrow Loch Eriboll

makes a deep indentation into the land, and I had now for several hours to coast round it on scarred roads. At the head of the loch are two great mountain peaks, less geometrically regular than the ones I had passed further south, but with the same solitary prominence, and as I drove slowly over the uneven stony surface I saw a huge cloud gathering over them. Presently a thick veil of rain came sweeping towards me over the intervening country. The sun was shining further to the west, and its rays cut a glittering swathe through the edge of the advancing rain, which at its centre was a black wall that grew taller and taller as it advanced, till it shut out the sky. I stopped the car, put up the hood, and lit a cigarette. Every living thing seemed to be waiting for that wave to sweep over it: the long grasses along the road were quite motionless; then I saw them trembling and waving beneath the soft gust of air that the wall of rain drove before it, and a moment afterwards a few drops pattered down: then a whole cataract descended on the roof of the car. The grasses, driven down flat, rebounded madly as if fighting for their life; shoots of light erratically pierced through the tumult of flying water from the sun still shining brightly somewhere behind the cloud; in a little while it shone in full force, though the fringes of the shower were still trailing past the hills. Then in a few minutes the air was quite hot and still again, and as I put up the hood a grey cloud of horse-flies descended on me. I hastily started the car to get rid of them, but I was to see more of them later on. I now had a clear view of the wild rocky outline of the east coast of Loch Eriboll, a tossing confusion of black bluffs, which gave an impression of panic flight as they swept outwards towards the open sea. It was the wildest, though not the strangest, scenery I had come to in the Highlands until now, and in that Sunday stillness, on the deserted road, it was a little frightening.

I was now approaching nearer and nearer to the two great peaks that guarded the head of the loch, and was presently running along a level road to the opposite side, through a marsh covered with tall grasses. Presently I came to a steep and long hill, up which I proceeded to jerk myself in the usual way. Here the horse-flies appeared again; they came in great numbers and floated past between me and the windscreen like a thin dangling moth-eaten veil. As soon as the car dropped to first gear they settled all over it and me. Both my hands were fully occupied in the complicated process of jerking the car up-hill. I went on as composedly as possible; but when I felt the horrible creatures crawling over my lips I became flustered, and just on the very top edge of the hill I pushed down the brake too hard and the car stopped. I flailed my arms through the air for a while and pushed the starter with my foot; but the engine would not start, so I got out and tinkered with the plugs in a cloud of horse-flies, which I tried to disperse by smoking one cigarette after another. At last a car appeared coming in the opposite direction, and the driver got down, unscrewed the plugs, did something or other to them, and started the car. I shall always feel grateful to him, whoever he was. In a little while I had jerked myself up to the top of the hill, where as if by general agreement the horse-flies turned back. It was on this hill that I must have tumbled off my suitcase, though I did not realize it until two hours later, when I reached Tongue. But by that time I was so terrified of the hills and the horse-flies that I would not have returned for a hundred pounds. So I reported the loss to the local constable, and duly received the suitcase, and all that was in it, quite unharmed, a fortnight later in Orkney.

But between Loch Eriboll and Tongue I had to pass through several more of these hot and breathless mountain valleys filled with horse-flies. The heat and the silence would have made these places sinister in any case, but the horse-flies intensified this impression immeasurably, perhaps because they were the same colour as the heather and looked like a dusty veil risen from it and armed with malignant power, an animate part of the landscape. In spite of the recent showers the air in these hollows had an arid burnt taste; and the dry, soft, almost gentle onset of these loathsome winged creatures was besides horribly deliberate. They seemed to gauge the speed of the car, know that when the road grew steep both my hands would be fully occupied, and calmly take advantage of the situation. To find these quite deserted valleys covered with horse-flies was also so strange that it gave me a superstitious feeling: for what blood could they find to suck in such places, all dead as the valley of bones?

I had tea at Tongue and lingered over it somewhat fearfully. But for the rest of my way I was not troubled with a single horse-fly. The road, too, was comparatively level, for the hills had receded. I passed a bay of beautiful white sand, and watched the Orkney Islands draw nearer in the bright evening light. After I had passed the little village of Bettyhill, where the road was filled with a black-coated crowd going to evening service, I overtook for the first time in my journey a car which was more down at heels than my own, driven somewhat apprehensively by two young men who looked like farm labourers. When I got to Melvich, a little village on the Pentland Firth, I decided to stop for the night, for it was by then after eight o'clock. As I was putting up my car at the garage the two young men appeared at it on foot: their car had broken down. Their apprehensions had been justified.

The evening I spent at Melvich was the pleasantest of all my journey. The hotel was unexpectedly comfortable and well-run, and the walls were quite without the usual bleeding array of pictured carcases. I had actually dreamt of a frieze of such walls one night in a hotel unusually well furnished with them; so that the relief with which I saw the clean walls of the Melvich Hotel, though it may seem excessive, was quite understandable to myself. I arrived long after dinner was over, but the lady who ran the place provided me with a better meal – cold chicken and dessert – than I had had in any of the other hotels. As I had only a drive of a dozen miles over a fairly level and good road next day, and this evening solemnized the end of my jerks, I decided to allow myself a bottle of wine, and was provided with a very good one. When I finished my dinner about half-past nine the light was still perfectly clear, so I went for a walk past the straggling houses of the little village until I came to the shore. The outlines of the Orkney hills were still distinct, and the evening had that perfect tranquillity which I have always associated for some reason with Sunday evenings, when the very quality of the light seems different. I wandered about the shore for some time in this strangely distinct and yet dream-like clarity. I stayed there until about eleven o'clock; watched the shadows of the cliffs motionlessly reflected in the sea, the Orkney hills blown like bubbles against the colourless sky, the horse and cattle near-by cropping the grass – the tearing of their teeth and the pounding of their hooves sounding strangely loud in that stillness and at that hour – and a few silent couples scattered here and there over the soft turf along the cliff-tops. When I turned in the outline of everything had become softer, but was still perfectly clear, and the windows of the houses gleamed brightly, appearing still to hold the fullness of the light after it had faded from the walls. At twelve o'clock as I was going to bed I looked out through the window of my room and saw some horses in a field still moving about restlessly in the light, and occasionally pawing the ground with their hooves. The outline of the Orkneys had almost faded away, and was like a dark breath on the horizon.

A Summing up

What is left to say when one has come to the end of writing about one's life? Some kind of development, I suppose, should be expected to emerge, but I am very doubtful of such things, for I cannot bring life into a neat pattern. If there is a development in my life – and that seems an idle supposition – then it has been brought about more by things outside than by any conscious intention of my own. I was lucky to spend my first fourteen years in Orkney; I was unlucky to live afterwards in Glasgow as a Displaced Person, until at last I acquired a liking for that plain, warm-hearted city. Because a perambulating revivalist preacher came to Kirkwall when I was a boy, I underwent an equivocal religious conversion there; because I read Blatchford in Glasgow, I repeated the experience in another form, and found myself a Socialist. In my late twenties I came, by chance, under the influence of Nietzsche. In my early thirties I had the good fortune to meet my wife, and have had since the greater good fortune of sharing my life with her. In my middle thirties I became aware of immortality, and realized that it gave me a truer knowledge of myself and my neighbours. Years later in St Andrews I discovered that I had been a Christian without knowing it. I saw in Czechoslovakia a whole people lost by one of the cruel turns of history, and exiled from themselves in the heart of their own country. I discovered in Italy that Christ had walked on the earth, and also that things truly made preserve themselves through time in the first freshness of their nature. Now and then during these years I fell into the dumps for short or prolonged periods, was subject to fears which I did not understand, and passed through stretches of blankness and deprivation. From these I learned things which I could not otherwise have learned, so that I cannot regard them as mere loss. Yet I believe that I would have been better without them.

When we talk of our development I fancy we mean little more than that we have changed with the changing world; and if we are writers or intellectuals, that our ideas have changed with the changing fashions of thought, and therefore not always for the better. I think that if any of us examines his life, he will find that most good has come to him from a few loyalties, and a few discoveries made many generations before he was born, which must always be made anew. These too may sometimes appear to come by chance, but in the infinite web of things and events chance must be something different from what we think it to be. To comprehend that is not given to us, and to think of it is to recognize a mystery, and to acknowledge the necessity of faith. As I look back on the part of the mystery which is my own life, my own fable, what I am most aware of is that we receive more than we can ever give; we receive it from the past, on which we draw with every breath, but also – and this is a point of faith – from the Source of the mystery itself, by the means which religious people call Grace.

LETTERS

to Sydney Schiff

the writer Stephen Hudson

St Andrews, 16 January, 1939

Dear Sydney,

Forgive me for not replying sooner. But Willa has been unwell; she has been ordered by the doctor to lie on her back and rest; her heart is weakened and missing its beat; and after her rest she must have a minor internal operation. I have been unwell too, and have had to have out all my remaining teeth but two; after this I shall be all right again. In the middle of all this, Gavin has had chickenpox; but that is a minor matter, and he is almost well again. But it has been a troubled time, and as far as Willa is concerned, still is. She has been overstraining her strength, it seems, for months.

Thanks for Broch's letter; Broch is a great man and a very good man. I don't know whether I agree or not with your opinion: that the only hope of the world lies in the gospel of Christ. As you know, I have believed for many years in the immortality of the soul; all my poetry springs from that in one form or another; and belief of that kind means belief in God, though my God is not that of the churches: and I can reconcile myself to no church. I have as little use for the materialist doctrines of Communism as you have, and Fascism seems to me definitely evil. I look upon myself as an anti-Marx socialist; a man who believes that people are immortal souls and that they should bring about on this earth a society fit for immortal souls. Immortality, unfortunately, does not make them good, and hardly any of them are conscious of immortality; they act for immediate and generally private and petty ends. Most of them no doubt have to do so for reasons of necessity: that should not be. I am quite clear in my mind that society must change, that Capitalism must be transcended; but if the change comes through the terrible Marxist machine of Materialist Determination, it will be a major calamity, for it denies the soul, and there cannot be a more fundamental denial than that. But everything is dark, and is getting darker: the horrible persecution of the Jews is the most obvious symptom of the madness which tinges all the new movement in Europe, but the movement itself threatens us all, and threatens everything that we not merely hold dear, but everything necessary for a real living life as apart from an ostensible one. There is a real denial of humanity here, as Broch says; there is more, a contempt for humanity, hatred of anyone with a separate, unique life of his own. The capacity to recognize immaterial realities is almost dead, it seems to me; is quite dead in the sphere of action at any rate, the sphere in which Hitler, Mussolini and Chamberlain move. And in the last resort we live by immaterial realities; that is our real life; the rest is more or less machinery. We are moved about, caught, wedged, clamped in this machinery; and that is what is called history.

I wish you both well and think often of you. I don't know when I shall see you again. I am as sick, I think, as you can be, over the dreadful things that are being done to the Jews, and the darkness that has fallen over them. I am ashamed, as every citizen in this country should be, of the part England has played. And I share, with everyone else, part of the responsibility for it; for we have all been too easy-going and thoughtless and hopeful.

My love to you both,

Edwin

Broch: *Hermann Broch, German writer, whose work Muir translated.*

to Joseph Chiari

poet and author of critical books

Dear Joe,

I am writing with great joy to tell you about a letter I got from *Orion* yesterday, accepting your longest poem . . .

My dear Joe, I can't tell you how delighted I am by this. I knew my own opinion of your poems, which I told you about in Edinburgh, but I knew also how various can be the opinion of writers about the same poetry and when I sent the poems to *Orion*, I simply did not know what to expect. And so you will appear first as a poet in what is really the best literary miscellany in Great Britain; and this is what I am so glad about.

Gavin has arrived at last; yesterday morning. I must thank you over and over again for all your kindness to him. Willa got Margaret's letter yesterday, and will reply to it to-day or to-morrow. We might have got both letters, Margaret's and the one from *Orion*, some days earlier, but we had been away in the Tatras, in the east of Slovakia, for a week, and just got back yesterday morning in time to meet Gavin's train. We went through some curious adventures to do that. Our car (or rather the Institute's car) had three punctures between the Tatras and Bratislava, where we arrived at 4 o'clock in the morning on Friday. Between Bratislava and Prague we had again three punctures, and were left without a spare wheel in lonely forest country early on Saturday morning: Gavin was going to arrive at the Wilson station in Prague, we were told, at 8 o'clock. We stopped a car that was passing, a huge car of a semi-racing type, and asked for a lift to Prague. The driver, a handsome, opulent-looking man, said he wasn't going to Prague, but that he could take us to Tabor (fifty miles from Prague), where we could get an early train to Prague that would get us there in good time. We both got in, leaving the chauffeur with the Institute car. The car into which we got was an open one. The driver set off at about 150 miles an hour. Willa was in front with him; I was in the back holding a jar of honey which we intended for Gavin's first breakfast with us; it had only a thin paper cover on the top. We came to various cross-roads marked Tabor, but in spite of what Willa said, the driver swept past them all, saying airily: 'Tabor! All roads lead to Tabor'. He took us at the same breakneck speed over half of Bohemia; it was quite dark, no moon; we passed through huge mountains, across great plains, round dizzy corners (still at about 150 miles an hour at least). Finally, when we found we were in quite a remote part of Bohemia, the driver shot past a car that was driving in front of us, and suddenly drew up across it, and asked for Tabor. We found we had to turn back for twenty miles; finally we arrived there after haring for more than three hours through the most wild and magnificent scenery, lit up brilliantly by the head lights. The driver (and he was a magnificent driver) was obviously half-mad and in command of a wonderful car; he was trying half to impress and half to terrify us; if we had shown any signs of alarm heaven knows to what lengths he might have gone. He turned every now and then to Willa and asked: 'Are you not afraid, gracious lady?', and when Willa said, 'No, why should I be afraid?' he was distinctly disappointed. At some points he would wave his hand negligently and say, 'I went over that wall once; the car was smashed to bits'; but he still failed to impress us; that is why he gave up at last in despair and actually took us to Tabor. Now and then he would take out a revolver, and tell us that he had been stopped by a man before he reached us; the man had asked for money, and he had shot between his legs, and rode away. The car as it leapt on bumped so furiously that the honey leapt up through the paper covering and was splashed over my trousers and all over the back seat; I was bathed in honey, and sitting on honey. Meanwhile I held the honey pot in my hands and decided just where I should hit the man on the head with it if he became really dangerous; I decided that behind the ear would be most effective. When we got to the Grand Hotel in Tabor, I aplogized for the honey spilt and smeared on the back seat, and the driver took out his revolver again and put it melodramatically to his head, and said to Willa: 'Honey on the back-seat: shall I shoot myself because of that, gracious lady?' Then we found that there was no early train from Tabor that would get us to Prague in time, and at this point Willa broke down and began to weep loudly. But there was a very nice nightwatchman in the hotel who took us in; I got out of my trousers, by now steeped in honey, and put on another pair; and the nightwatchman managed to get us a taxi (between four and five in the morning), and on that we set out on the fifty mile stretch to Prague, and arrived at last. As soon as I arrived I had a bath to get the honey off me; I'm not sure whether it is all off yet, for it sticks like anything. And so that is our most curious adventure since we came to Czechoslovakia. I should have mentioned that while we were going at this incredible speed, the driver had a habit of taking both hands off the wheel to gesticulate or make one of his silly remarks or to light a cigarette. The curious thing about this Walküre ride was that it was extraordinarily exhilarating, in spite of being alarming; I hadn't known what speed was before; it is something that literally carries you away, so that you aren't in the least concerned when you turn a sharp corner with all the tyres screaming on two wheels. Willa felt exactly the same, she told me after (We hadn't time to compare notes while the hurricane drive was on. Actually the man told her that he was going to take part in a race two days afterwards). No, the only thing that really alarmed us was the man himself, his shouts, his whistles and hoots, his remarks and his revolver.

We are a little bit exhausted after these strong sensations, and want nothing more than to remain motionless, and rest. My dear Joe, I still feel so happy about the poem. I see I haven't mentioned the name of the man I got the letter from; it is Denys Kilham Roberts, the remaining editor, along with myself, if I am still regarded as one of the editors. I do hope you will keep up your poetry, whenever the mood seizes you. I like your poems very much, as you know. Will I try some of the others on John Lehmann, whom I know? And have you written any more? I want to thank you again for all you have done for Gavin. We intend to keep him here until the beginning of October, when the new term begins: I think it would be foolish for him to return for that examination in the beginning of September; and he needs our care for some time. He arrived perfectly all right, and enjoyed the experience, though it rather alarmed him in prospect: it has been very good for him. I shall write to you again soon. With thanks again and love to Margaret and yourself, not forgetting the children. I am typing this, for my writing, I know, is an infliction on my friends, Give my kindest regards to the Orrs. I'm very very sorry that Harry Wood has been ill; do give him my kind regards too, and the hope that he will soon be better.

Yours ever,
Edwin

Letter from *Orion: from D. Kilham Roberts, expressing admiration for Chiari's 'White Temple by the Sea' and accepting it for publication in* Orion IV.
Institute: *British Council Institute of which Muir was Director (1945–8).*
Orrs: *Professor John Orr of Edinburgh University and his French wife.*

to Alec Aitken

Reader, later Professor of Mathematics at Edinburgh University

Newbattle, 28 June, 1951

Dear Alec,

Forgive me for not writing sooner; the last term with all the students always on my door-step, or in my room (nice, quite delightful students, but so continually there!), visitors, reports, God knows what, quite wore me out, and as soon as the term ended I had to go down to London to attend to some personal as well as college things. But your last intensely interesting letter (which I shall treasure) could not be resisted. My dear Alec, how are you now? I feel you are greatly better, and I'm so glad. Is it possible for you to come out and see us some day, now that this morning promises good weather again? Do come and let us talk about the universe: if nothing else, I'll listen.

I think you made too much of my broadcast. I was trying to draw a simple distinction, corresponding to the distinction which we make normally between 'imaginative literature' and 'science'. I was perhaps unfair to science, not knowing nearly enough about it. But I was concerned with the power which produces for us a *picture* of the world and human life, in which everything moves and is individual; and imaginative literature (and the imaginative arts) alone does that. It is necessary for us to have a picture, an image of our life, if our life is to be of any significance; and my complaint is that the ability to produce the picture is declining, and that when it is produced it tends more and more to be confused and inconclusive; and one of the reasons I put down for this (perhaps wrongly) was that the mental energy of mankind had gone more and more into the pursuit of knowledge, more and more exact, about such things as the universe. You write in your letter, my dear Alec, about the universe; but I want to know something about Tom and Dick and Jane, and their relations to one another as they move about; I want to know something, too, about myself, my moods, my relation within myself to everything as it impinges *immediately* upon me (and that is always). This wish, followed out, creates a picture of life, or a series of pictures, drawn from experience and intuition (never demonstrable). The picture is humanly necessary and can never be complete. It has to be visual, sensible, and as far as it comes from participation in life, as far as it shows understanding, spiritual at the same time. That, I suppose, is what one understands by imaginative literature. The wider our knowledge of ourselves, the world and the universe, of course, the more sublime the picture will be. Dante was fortunate in living at a time when it was still possible to have a *pictorial* vision of the universe, with Jerusalem at its centre, and all lines radiating out from that. Science did not exist then for itself, or literature for itself, or business for itself; but all had their central point, their Jerusalem, which was the queen of sciences, Theology. But things, as Yeats said, have fallen apart since then; the centre does not hold; and we hardly know, except by an isolated act of faith, where the centre is. And it does not help me, as a human being finding his way between birth and death, to know that the universe is not the material construction erected by nineteenth-century science. I am glad it is not; I never believed it, in any case. But this life is what concerns me, and is what concerns the imagination as I conceive it, the immediate life of sensation, feeling, divination, attraction, repulsion, enjoyment, suffering, with whatever meaning can be wrung out of it (and meaning it has, perhaps too many meanings). Science is a wonderful thing – I realize this, for I know you and can guess at your experience of it; guess at but not know, for my experience of life does not come to me through science but through the often blind gropings of an imperfect imagination.

And great as science is, I am troubled by the thought (often expressed) that knowledge means power, and that power falls into the hands of scoundrels and fanatics. It seems to me a real problem, and the problem of our time. Take the example of Communism. The Communist revolution should have happened in the second half of last century. There would have been 'revolutions', in Marx's sense, in the various capitals of Europe, not much more destructive than a

Saturday night riot in a provincial town. But now Communism is breaking the world in two; to put it to the test would be like flinging a match into a powder magazine; it would blow us all up and the world along with us. For we have so much knowledge of things, and so little knowledge of ourselves. I am trying to gratify my plea for imagination, and my conviction that our development for the last 3 or 4 centuries has been a lop-sided one.

I think you put words in my mouth in talking about imagination as 'the mind free to create'. I'm not much concerned with imaginative 'creation', but rather with true and false imagination. Most of 'doodling' is false, though it can be of use in leading one to something more genuine. I've never had any use for 'surrealism', though some writers have come to something more real by passing through that phase: Dylan Thomas, for instance. But, my dear Alec, what do you mean by saying so mysteriously that I am being weighed in the balance? Aren't we all, and the world along with us? And what is the *verdict*, with its [?] harshness, that you cannot give me? I have never bothered much about my reputation, such as it is. But in the last few years more young writers have written about me than ever before (and the young ones particularly) and quite recently a young poet I had never met wrote asking if he could bring out a collected edition of my poetry with an introduction by himself. It was quite unexpected and touching, and Fabers *are* bringing the book out. Really all this does not affect me very much, though I feel surprised and glad that the young writers should like my work so much better than my contemporaries did. But what does it matter, in any case? We shall pass, and our works with us. Yet I should very much like to know that verdict. And do come and see us.

Yours affectionately
Edwin Muir

Aitken had written about Muir's broadcast talk 'The Decline of the Imagination', which was published in the Listener *on 10 May. In the next number of the* Listener *two correspondents challenged Muir's views, and he answered on 24 May defending his sharp distinction between imagination and science. The scientist strives towards exact knowledge, whereas imagination 'can never arrive at exact knowledge, since it deals with things, and highly important things, about which exact knowledge does not exist.' See also his essay 'The Poetic Imagination' in the second edition of* Essays on *Literature and Society (1965).*

ENVOI

Edwin Muir at Newbattle

We never thought there could be writers in our islands. Writers were people who lived in cities and far-away places. The islands were for farmers and fishermen and shopkeepers.

We found, later, from the anthology *The Orkney Book* (1909) that indeed there had been nineteenth-century Orkney poets, Vedder and Malcolm. But there was something faded and third-hand about their verse, imitations of Byron.

Then the name of a new writer was mentioned: Eric Linklater. *Whitemaa's Saga* gripped my imagination at once; so, soon, did *The Men of Ness* and *Magnus Merriman*. Here were fields and shores that we actually knew, our feet had walked on them. Recognizable people came to life, and suffered and laughed out of the pages. It was a marvellous experience, reading the early Linklater; it was as if at once the common landscapes and seascapes became precious to us. That richness has never been lost.

But then Eric Linklater began to set his scenes in the great world – America, China – and that did not mean so much. But still, again and again, he gave short story or essay or fragment of autobiography an Orkney setting, and the magic was astir again.

I knew, vaguely, the name of another writer – Edwin Muir – but his books were a long time in getting to us. Also, he was an Orcadian only by birth; he lived mostly in Scotland and England, or in Europe with his wife Willa.

Sometime in the mid-forties I read the first version of his auto-biography, *The Story and the Fable*. The opening – Muir's childhood in the island of Wyre, among the farm folk and animals and the ripening corn – still seems to me to be one of the most beautiful evocations of innocence and of the slow stainings and renewings of time in the language.

His poems appeared from time to time in the *Listener*. They were strange and baffling, and yet they had (it seemed) a secret and exact music. It required patience to understand such poetry. Muir's volume *The Voyage* came out in 1946. As if a key had been turned in a door, I entered a chamber of pure lyrical meditation. Poem after poem enchanted me: 'The Return', 'The Castle', 'Thought and Image', 'The Rider Victory', 'The Transmutation', 'In Love for Long'.

I used to enjoy those great poems over and over again, in Kirkwall, with Ernest Marwick and Robert Rendall and a few friends. Some other poems, it's true, baffled us with the density of their images.

But we had found a new hero, and one moreover who had drawn the nourishment for his poetry from his childhood in Orkney. Even the texture of the verse had the grainings of Orkney in it: its shape mirrored the quiet flowing laterals of the Orkney fields and hills.

In 1951 I was given the opportunity to attend Newbattle Abbey College, 8 miles from Edinburgh, for a session.

Edwin Muir was in Orkney that summer with his wife. He invited me for afternoon tea in Stromness Hotel. I remember chiefly the flow of Willa's talk and laughter; she loved life and the masquers in the pageant of life and chiefly the amusing ways they behave. Edwin sat, smiling and smoking cigarettes for the most part. He had large blue eyes, full sensuous lips, freckled hands. He told me, kindly, that he had read one of my short stories that the *New Shetlander* had recently published. He would be happy, he said, to enrol me as a student at Newbattle when the new session began in October – Edwin had been appointed Warden the previous year.

To me, who had never been so far south before, it was an adventure. Edwin Muir met me off the train at Waverley one Sunday afternoon, and drove me to Newbattle; the trees were rich with autumn.

The students arrived, about a score of them, in the next few days.

They were mostly young working men and women from Scotland, but a few came from England and further afield. There ought to have been about sixty students, but local authorities were reluctant to give grants to students who wouldn't be called upon to sit exams and so 'improve themselves'. For such people, Newbattle was a kind of indulgence. Poetry, philosophy – what relevance had such things to the stern real world of 1951? Yet these young men and women, on meagre grants, had left secure jobs for this one opportunity in their lives to drink at the pure springs.

Edwin Muir, during his years as Warden, had to fight this perpetual rearguard action against a committee of stern no-nonsense men. In the end, he was glad to break out of it. But those few years that he was Warden of Newbattle are remembered with gratitude by the students who sat under him.

Edwin Muir lectured two or three times a week. He would enter the room in a kind of slow glide, nod amiably to us, sit at his desk and begin to talk impromptu about Marlowe, Chapman, Shakespeare. (That year the course of lectures was on the Elizabethan dramatists.) The opening words were vague and dreamlike, full of hesitations and gropings for phrases. Then he would warm to his theme, and the rock was struck, and the felicitous argument came easily and naturally. Whenever he had to read a piece from the play, or consult a scrap of note, off would come his glasses, and then it could be seen how large and blue his eyes were . . . The lecture flowed on, without vulgar emphasis or gesture, till it reached its inevitable pellucid close.

Because there was no declamation or false emphasis, a few of the students were disappointed. Most of us knew that we had been sitting for an hour beside pure springs.

Edwin had never lost his Orkney accent, though his family had moved from Orkney to Glasgow half-a-century before.

For another hour in the week he instructed us in the writing of English. This was a more pedestrian exercise. He was concerned that we should write simple plain English, saying what we wanted to say, neither more nor less: the construction of sentences and paragraphs, and where commas and semi-colons should be set to point, felicitously, the meaning. Beyond the plain English, if there was to be any flowering, it would come at its own time, and it would be in each instance a different kind of flowering.

He received us, one by one, with our written essay, in his wide study looking out over the Italian garden and the ancient beech-tree and the stone sundial, in which time was cut and angled so marvellously in eight shifting facets.

The occasional essay could consist of anything: verse, story, fragment of autobiography, criticism. Edwin sat, with swirls of cigarette smoke about his head, and was kind to all our manuscripts. (Some of them must have been pretty dreadful.) There would be silent periods, while warden and student looked out across the garden and the hidden river Esk flowing past the Abbey. Then the trance would be broken, and Edwin would dismiss the essayist with a few kind encouraging phrases. But Tom Wilson, one of the students, used to say that you could always tell whether or not Edwin had really liked the essay by the tone of voice in which he said in valediction, 'Oh yes . . . I liked it.'

Willa's presence was felt everywhere in the college: cheerful, kind, delighted especially if she succeeded in slightly shocking someone. But there was never malice in her laughter. She was the most generous woman I have ever known. She would tutor this student and that in Latin (for no reward, I'm sure). Once I was unwell, and she installed me in the guest bedroom of her flat, so that I could recover with delicious meals and peace and laughter and good books . . . Yet all the time we were at Newbattle she herself was far from well, with arthritis; she toiled along laboriously on a stick. Edwin too had occasional bad times, mainly with his delicate stomach; no doubt conflicts in high places about the future of Newbattle fretted him.

There was little morbidity in the parties the Muirs gave in their flat. Willa's heartiness infected everyone, even the shy students. She kept the wine flowing, and our plates full of savouries and cakes: a bounteous never-silent provider. On those occasions, Edwin sat in a corner taking tiny sips from his wine-glass, silent and gentle and smiling, as if part of him was in another world.

Snow came. (In Orkney, I had never known such intense preparatory frost.) On the far bank of the Esk, we cut down trees and sawed them into logs for the fire in the Abbey crypt. The winter evenings, after dinner, were spent by the students in the crypt, with political talk, and books and papers, and often on a Saturday evening, (after beer in the Justinlees Inn) impromptu poetry recitals. When the fire burned low, Jimmy Jarvie would say, 'Put another peasant on the fire'. And more logs would be set on the lessening flames.

I have not, before or since, known such friendship. In the Justin-lees bar a mile up the road, at Eskbank, beer never tasted so good.

We scared each other, or pretended to, with stories of the Abbey ghosts on the ancient worn spiral stair, and in the billiard room next the crypt. The ghosts added a dark tremble to the winter joys.

We all dispersed for Christmas. I remember getting off the aeroplane at Kirkwall and going to a bar in Kirkwall for a pint of bass. The full wonderment of the winter term at Newbattle broke on me as the yellow circles lessened in the pint glass.

In January, when we returned to the Abbey, there was a great storm that blew down the ancient beech tree beyond the garden.

Places further north had taken the full fury of the storm. Orkney was scourged from end to end; everything standing and vulnerable was beaten flat, and hen-houses full of fluttering panic were blown out to sea. Edwin listened entranced as stories of storm damage came in from the north; no doubt he remembered the wild gale-swept nights of his childhood on the farm – 'now the wind whips the pane!'

In the crypt he joined us, students and staff, for mid-morning tea or coffee. We stood around, in little groups; Edwin spoke little but listened to everyone, smoking his cigarette and smiling amiably.

Then suddenly, in the heart of winter, the heating failed. The Abbey was slowly drained of warmth. We washed and shaved shiveringly in cold water. (Five centuries before, winter must have been like this to the monks.) We clustered about the crypt fire like wasps round an emptying jam-pot. In the library we turned pages with long blue fingers. How long did this Ice Age last? A few days only, I think. The fault in the furnace was repaired; warmth flowed back through the intricate ancient stonework. We turned our thawed-out intelligences once more to the contemplation of Shakespeare and Marlowe, Dickens and Shelley and Yeats.

On Friday mornings in the English class there was a seminar, in which a student would read a paper on any subject of his choice, and then have it subjected to criticism and analysis by the other students. Edwin presided over those sessions, a kind presence. (He never said or did anything, in my experience, to hurt anyone, as if something delicate might be damaged or destroyed.) The thought of reading a paper at the seminar was a fearful thing to me. In the end Edwin read to the class an essay I wrote on the ballads, while I lay in bed, feigning sickness.

But the bitter cold of that winter put a real illness on me at last. It drained the vital cheerful spirits out of me; the world (even Newbattle Abbey) was a grey place for weeks. The thought of travelling to Orkney during the Easter break was a burden. In the end my friend and fellow-student Ian MacArthur invited me to spend Easter with his brother and sister-in-law in Paisley. In that grey town, among much laughter and generosity, I quickly recovered.

We returned eagerly to Newbattle for the summer term.

That spring and summer was one of the happiest times in my life. Trees in Orkney are a rarity; here was suddenly foliage, sweet tall green cloaks everywhere, sylvan groups and congregations. The roadside, going steeply up to Eskbank, was lyrical with lilac, juniper, apple-blossom. (Only the River Esk, that should have gone a blue singing thread through the green tapestry, ran turbid and mud-coloured; because, it was said, of the mills up-stream.)

It is usual, I suppose, for young people to be happy at that time of the year. Yet I think there would not have been such a delightful atmosphere in the college had it not been that Edwin and Willa Muir ruled with gentleness and charity and kindness from the centre. Their presences threw no shadow across our days, but only light, and made more meaningful our communings with books and the spring-time and our friends.

In those beautiful mornings of April and May, 1952, we would see Edwin and Willa walking together in the garden or beside the river. Willa toiled along slowly on her stick, in constant pain because of arthritis. Edwin walked beside her in a slow trance-like glide.

The birds flew and sang from tree to tree, and the days lengthened, and the sun got brighter.

Quite often, all through the session, there would be recitals in the magnificent drawing room on the first floor. This room, when first I saw it, took my breath with the sheer beauty of it: the splendour of the high azure-and-gold ceiling, the walls lined with Van Dycks, the magnificent grand piano in one corner. In this peerless room, on certain evenings, musicians came from Edinburgh and performed for us. Often the Muirs' only son, Gavin, a brilliant musician, gave recitals on the grand piano. Gavin's fine intellect and artistry were denied full flowering by an almost total deafness, the result of an accident in London in his childhood. Gavin lived all that year in the Abbey, in his parents' flat. He (himself young) mingled well with the students; urging every political argument, in the crypt or the Justinlees, a little to the left; but few arguments ended in acrimony, for laughter and good fellowship were everywhere that year. We existed in an idyll. It was impossible that any Malvolio or Iago would come and sour the scene.

In the summer mornings mist would lie in the valley of the Esk; then, towards noon, the sun would break through, and Edwin would give his lecture in some outside nook or coign of the Abbey. That is one lingering memory: Edwin discussing, with the slight 'burr' in his voice, the world's great books – *The Symposium*, *Don Quixote*, and others – while his students sat round him in the grass, and the birds sang, and bees foraged in the flowers.

In mid-May we, who had been such a happy company, began to realize that time was running out for us fast; the idyll was almost over.

The *Listener* carried a poem by Edwin one week, one of the most beautiful lyrics he ever wrote, 'The Late Swallow'. I read it (as far as I remember) at the breakfast table, and was deeply impressed by the imagery, the movement – made memorable by the rhymed interweaving of short and long lines – the perfect workmanship. I told Willa how much I admired it. 'It is Edwin's epitaph,' she said.

The college broke up on the thirteenth June, 1952. That same day, Edwin Muir's *Collected Poems* was published by Faber. I saw, with interest and joy, that the quality of the poems improved with every new page. Here was a poet who, starting late, had kept the best of his work for his old age, like Thomas Hardy and Sophocles.

Edwin and Willa said farewell to us at the great door of the Abbey.

Pledging each other eternal friendship, we went our separate ways home, but bearing with us the radiance of one brief year.

Inevitably, our letters got shorter and more infrequent over the years; and now only a few of that score of students are in touch with each other, and that rarely.

Edwin Muir was to live for another six and a half years. He had disappointments, especially when the work and function of the college was criticized in high places. In the end he resigned. His health was always uncertain. But he and Willa had great happiness in America, where he was invited to give the Charles Eliot Norton lectures at Harvard. From across the Atlantic his kindness reached to me; he got some of my poems published in *Harper's Bazaar*. Nearer home, he later (unknown to me) sent a sheaf of my verse to The Hogarth Press: and so I got hardback publication without any effort on my part – a unique experience in literature, I should think. Such kindness and concern by a famous writer for a quite unknown one must be extremely rare. By myself, I should never have dared to send a manuscript to a publisher.

So, for that and for much besides, I am grateful to him, and (with many others who were young in those days) I honour the memory of a good and greatly gifted man.

Every life, like every civilization, has its golden age. My good time was the few months between October 1951 and June 1952.

Reading over this account of Edwin Muir, it strikes me that I have not drawn a true portrait of him. What was this mild amiable smiling presence who drifted for a few years through the corridors and garden paths of Newbattle Abbey? Not Edwin Muir. What is not evident in the article is an inner resilient core of toughness – only that could have saved him from the clash of two cultures that killed, in a very short time, four of his family after they moved to Glasgow. No one becomes a poet and critic of his stature who isn't possessed of an unwavering dedication. These aspects of E.M. are not apparent in the above – I note it with some shame.

Perhaps I should have mentioned, too, that he had an aversion to speaking about his own work; an unusual thing in a poet. Images and symbols that occur over and over in his poetry he would not allow to be trotted out in discussion; their place is in the Temple of Poetry only – Eden, the Fall, etc.

GMB

Index